W9-AXV-764

UPDATED!
SUPER
WINGS

THE STEP-BY-STEP PAPER AIRPLANE BOOK

BY PETER CLEMENS
Additional illustrations by Jose Delgado

Copyright © 1996 by RGA Publishing Group, Inc.

All rights reserved. No part of this book may be reproduced or transmitted in any form or by any means, electronic or mechanical, including photocopying and recording, or by any information storage or retrieval system, except as may be expressly permitted by the 1976 Copyright Act or in writing by the publisher.

Requests for such permissions should be addressed to:

Lowell House Juvenile

2020 Avenue of the Stars, Suite 300

Los Angeles, CA 90067

Lowell House books can be purchased at special discounts when ordered in bulk for premiums and special sales. Contact Department JH at the above address.

Manufactured in the United States of America

ISBN: 1-56565-536-2

10 9 8 7 6 5 4 3 2 1

INTRODUCTION

SUPER WINGS is your guide to making and flying paper airplanes. There are hundreds of paper airplane designs. To get you started, here are nineteen fun and easy models. You will soon discover the fun of launching a neatly folded plane that you have made yourself out of nothing more than paper, tape, and paper clips.

Every model in this book is simple to make, and most of them require only a few minutes of work.

8½"x 11" paper	A ruler	Thread
8½"x 14" paper	A box of paper clips	A small toy
A pair of scissors	A plastic straw	A hobby knife
A roll of cellophane tape	A two-ply paper dinner napkin	Thin cardboard

Here is what you will need:

Colored construction paper	Origami paper	Colored pencils
Colored typing paper	Markers	

Optional:
AERODYNAMICS

There are four basic forces that work together to make something fly. They act the same way on a bird, an airplane, a flying squirrel, or anything else that flies. These four forces are thrust, lift, gravity, and drag.

Thrust is the force that moves something forward through the air.

When something is moving forward, the air flowing over and under it creates **lift. Lift** keeps the object in the air.

Gravity is the force that tries to pull all flying objects back to earth. Gravity works against **lift.**

When something is flying through the air, the air it is traveling through acts like an anchor and slows the object down. This force is called **drag.** If you have ever tried to run through water, you know what the **drag** of the water against your legs feels like.

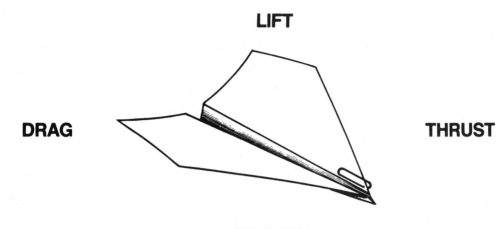

LIFT

DRAG

THRUST

GRAVITY

When you design a paper airplane, you have to balance the **lift** and the **thrust** so that they will be stronger than **gravity** and the **drag** of the air. If you have done your job well, your plane will fly. If you have not, it will probably spin to the ground and crash. If this happens, don't be discouraged. As you practice more, your original designs will become better.

FOLDING AND LAUNCHING

One of the secrets to making successful paper airplanes is to make all folds neat and sharp. Be as careful and accurate as you can. You can start some of the more difficult ones by bending the paper over a ruler.

When you launch your airplane, you are going to provide the **thrust** needed for it to fly. Hold the "fuselage," the central body of the airplane, in your hand. Then move your whole arm forward and let go. Do not throw the plane into the air. Make sure that the nose is pointed slightly down, instead of straight ahead.

On some of the planes, like the design on page 13, small tabs are cut into the back edges of the wings and turned up slightly. These are called "elevators." Their job is to provide balance to those designs that have extra weight in the nose. Experiment with the amount you bend up these elevators until the plane flies well.

Have fun!

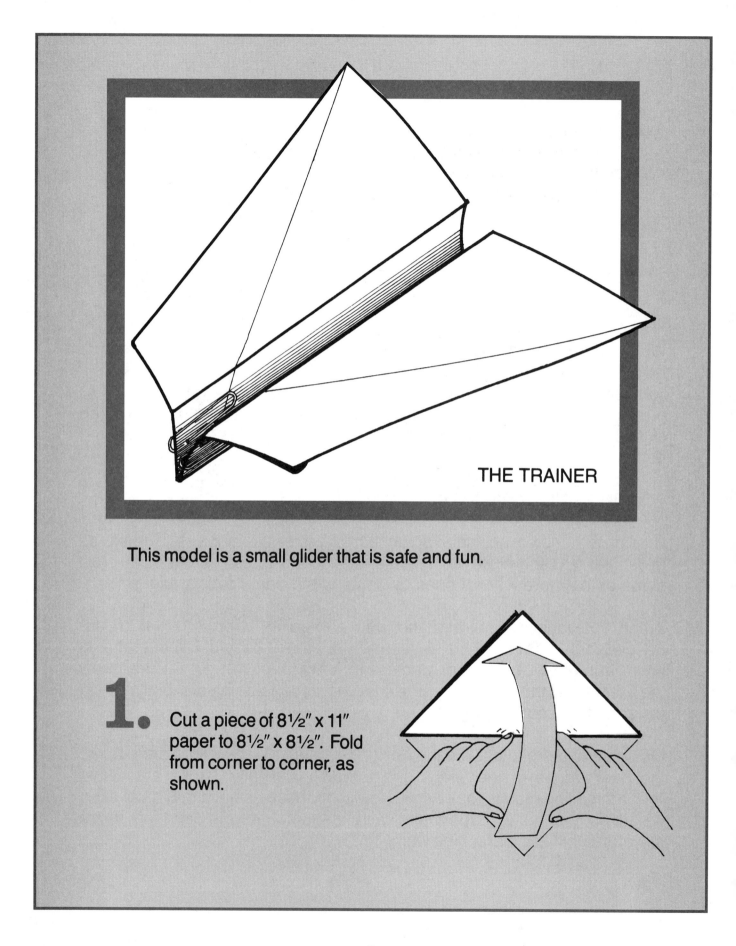

THE TRAINER

This model is a small glider that is safe and fun.

1.

Cut a piece of 8½" x 11" paper to 8½" x 8½". Fold from corner to corner, as shown.

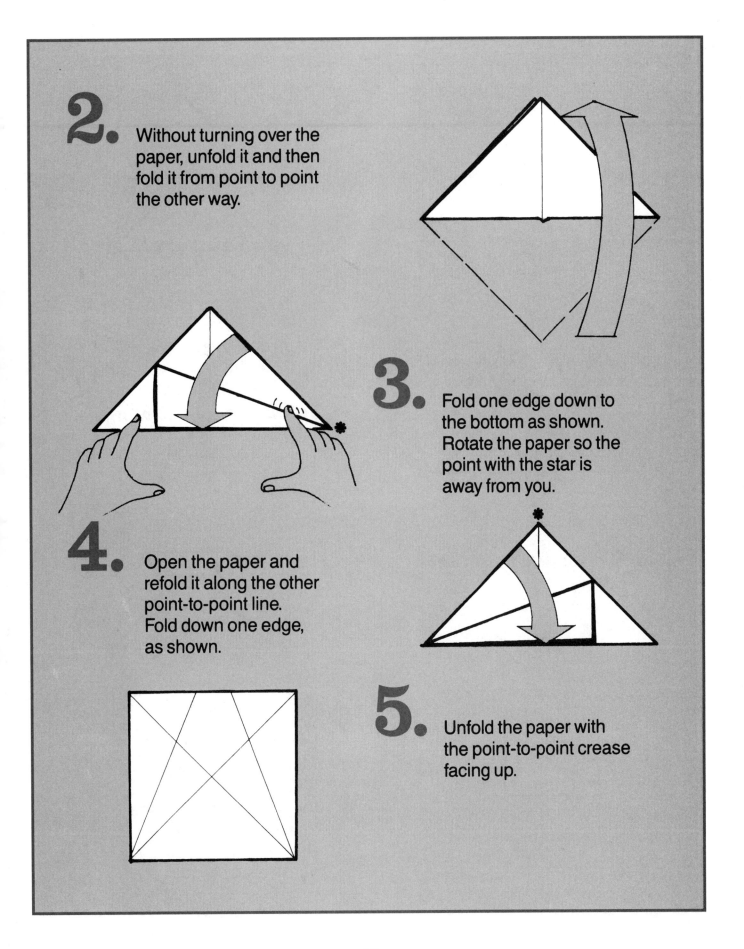

2. Without turning over the paper, unfold it and then fold it from point to point the other way.

3. Fold one edge down to the bottom as shown. Rotate the paper so the point with the star is away from you.

4. Open the paper and refold it along the other point-to-point line. Fold down one edge, as shown.

5. Unfold the paper with the point-to-point crease facing up.

6. Fold in along the other creases like this.

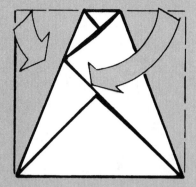

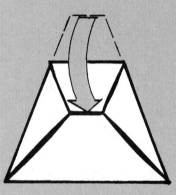

7. Fold the top down (about 2½") so that the two points touch the other edges as shown in the diagram on the left.

8. Fold down to those points again.

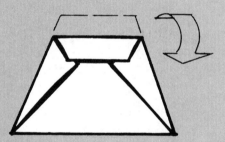

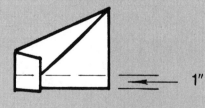

1″

9. Turn over your design. Fold the plain sides together, as shown. Measure 1″ for the fuselage and fold down the wings to look like the finished sketch on page 4. Add two paper clips and you're ready to go!

THE FLOATING SEMI-WING

This model looks like a shorter, wider version of the classic dart-shaped paper airplane but is actually quite different. You can launch it hard, straight up and it will float down in big lazy circles.

1. Fold an 8½″ x 11″ piece of paper in half the long way.

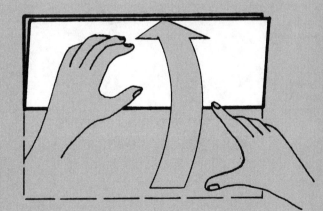

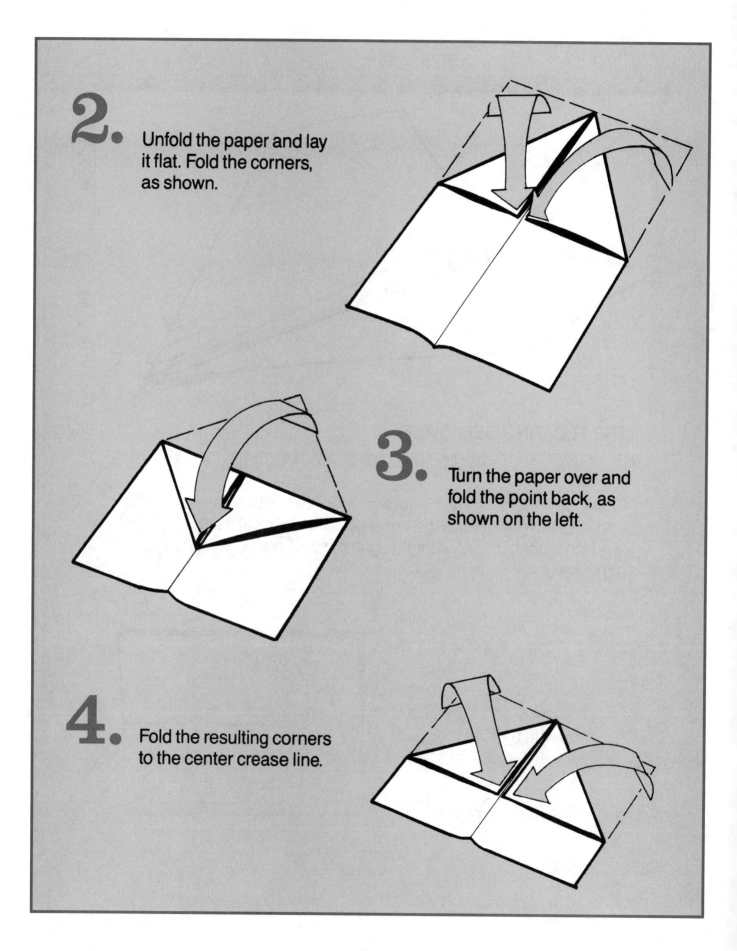

2. Unfold the paper and lay it flat. Fold the corners, as shown.

3. Turn the paper over and fold the point back, as shown on the left.

4. Fold the resulting corners to the center crease line.

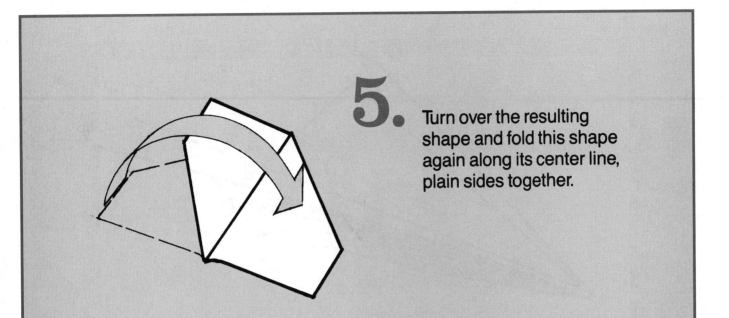

5. Turn over the resulting shape and fold this shape again along its center line, plain sides together.

6. Lay it down like this. Measure 1¼" up from the bottom and make a mark. Tape the bottom.

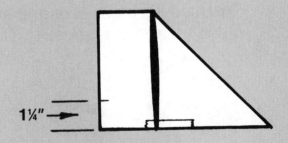

1¼" →

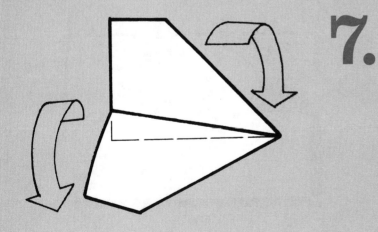

7. Fold both wings down along a line connecting this mark and the nose. Unfold it to look like the finished sketch on page 7. Add a paper clip and you're ready to go flying!

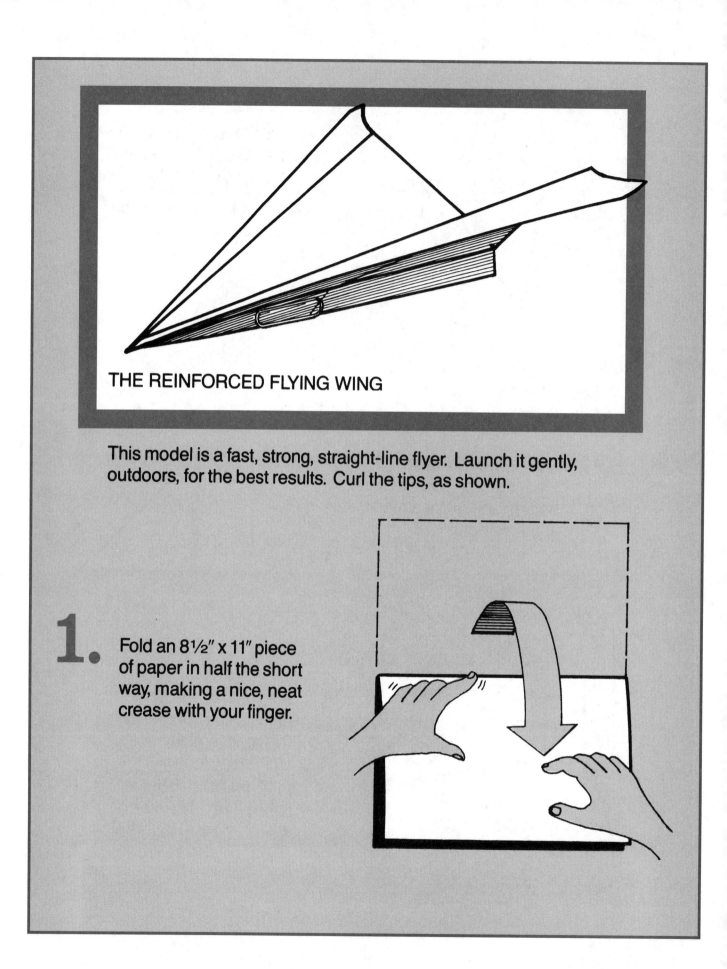

THE REINFORCED FLYING WING

This model is a fast, strong, straight-line flyer. Launch it gently, outdoors, for the best results. Curl the tips, as shown.

1. Fold an 8½" x 11" piece of paper in half the short way, making a nice, neat crease with your finger.

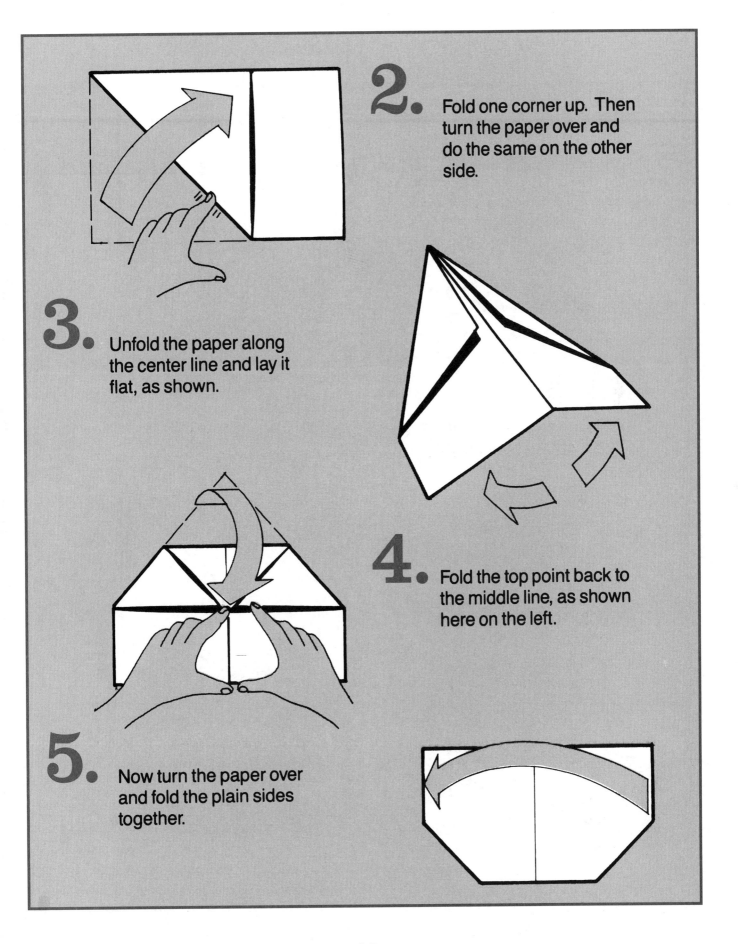

2. Fold one corner up. Then turn the paper over and do the same on the other side.

3. Unfold the paper along the center line and lay it flat, as shown.

4. Fold the top point back to the middle line, as shown here on the left.

5. Now turn the paper over and fold the plain sides together.

6. Lay the paper flat in this position.

7. Fold so that the corner with the star comes down to where the other folds meet. Repeat on the other side.

8. Tape in place with cellophane tape. Measure one inch from the top and bottom and make a mark.

1"

1"

9. Fold from each mark to the nose. Add a paper clip to the bottom. Unfold and adjust to look like the sketch on page 10.

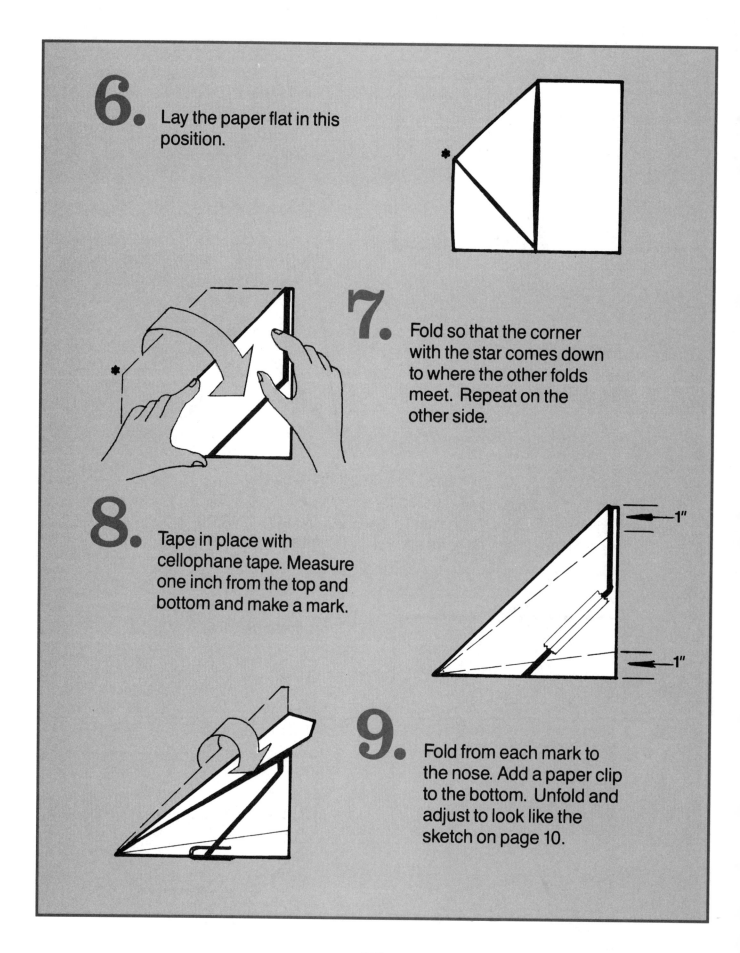

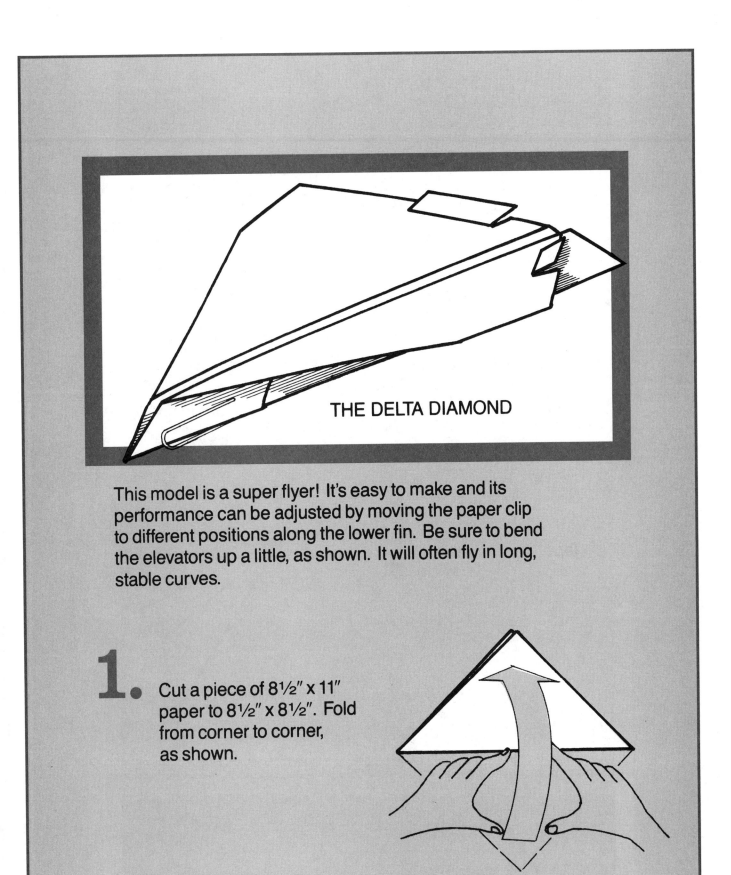

THE DELTA DIAMOND

This model is a super flyer! It's easy to make and its performance can be adjusted by moving the paper clip to different positions along the lower fin. Be sure to bend the elevators up a little, as shown. It will often fly in long, stable curves.

1. Cut a piece of 8½″ x 11″ paper to 8½″ x 8½″. Fold from corner to corner, as shown.

2. Fold one edge down to meet the crease.

3. Flip the paper over toward you and do the same to the other side.

4. Now open the paper and lay it flat so that you have this:

5. Fold the point to where the other corners meet.

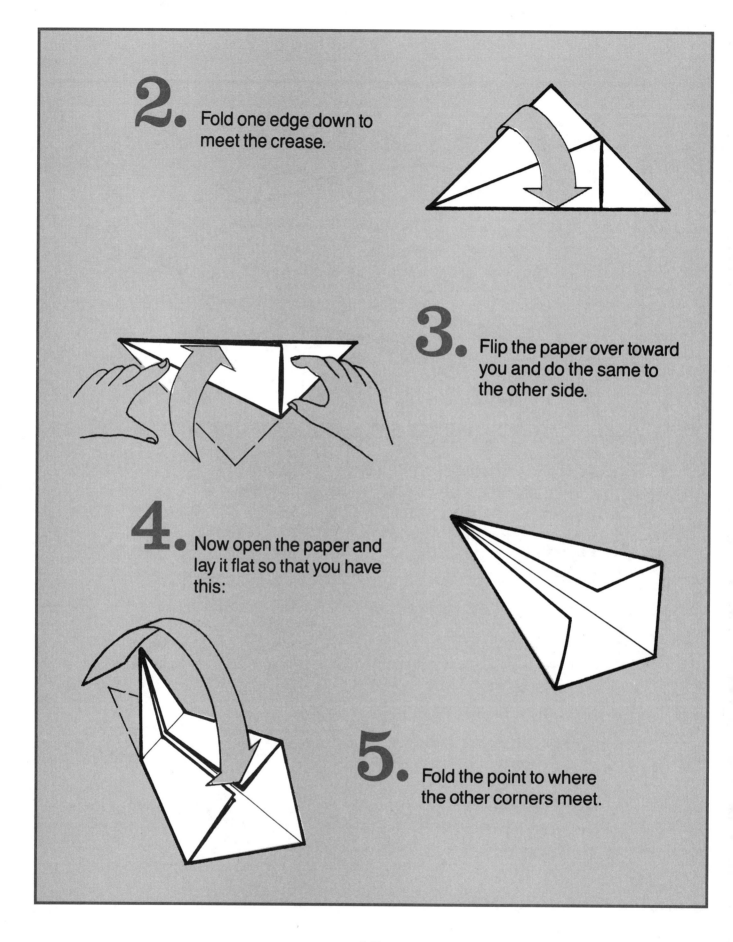

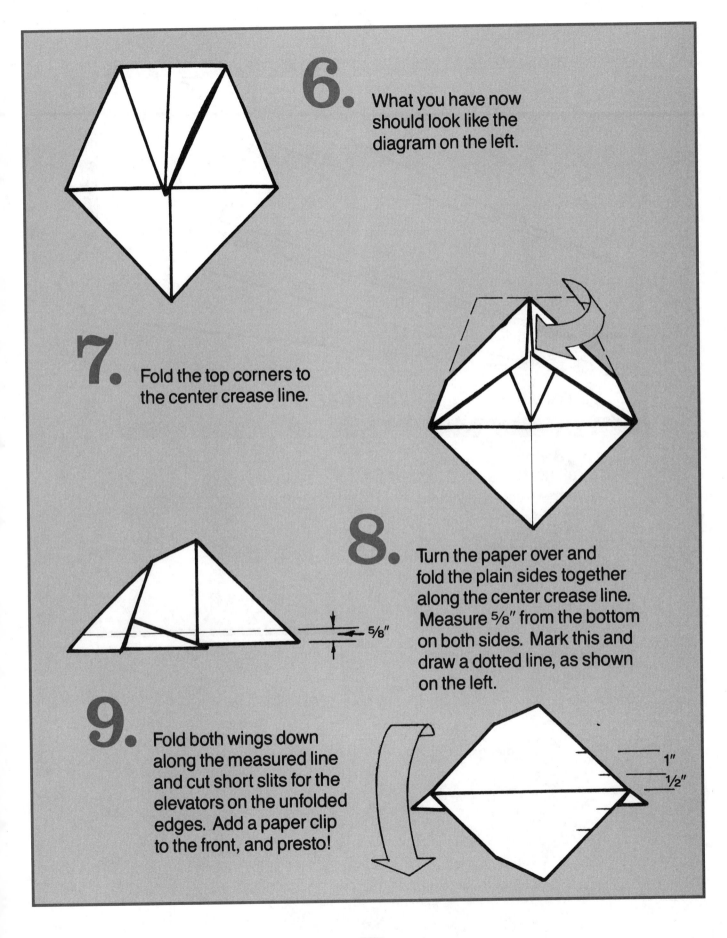

6. What you have now should look like the diagram on the left.

7. Fold the top corners to the center crease line.

8. Turn the paper over and fold the plain sides together along the center crease line. Measure ⅝" from the bottom on both sides. Mark this and draw a dotted line, as shown on the left.

5/8"

9. Fold both wings down along the measured line and cut short slits for the elevators on the unfolded edges. Add a paper clip to the front, and presto!

1"
½"

THE PARALLEL FOLD BUMBLE BEE

This plane looks like a big fat bee with its wings folded, but it is one of the best flying designs in this book. It may or may not require a paper-clip nose weight.

1. Fold an 8½" x 11" piece of paper in half the long way.

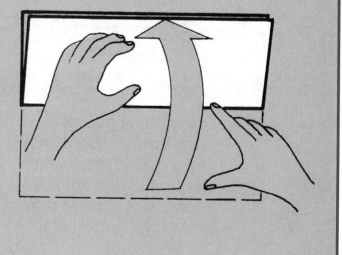

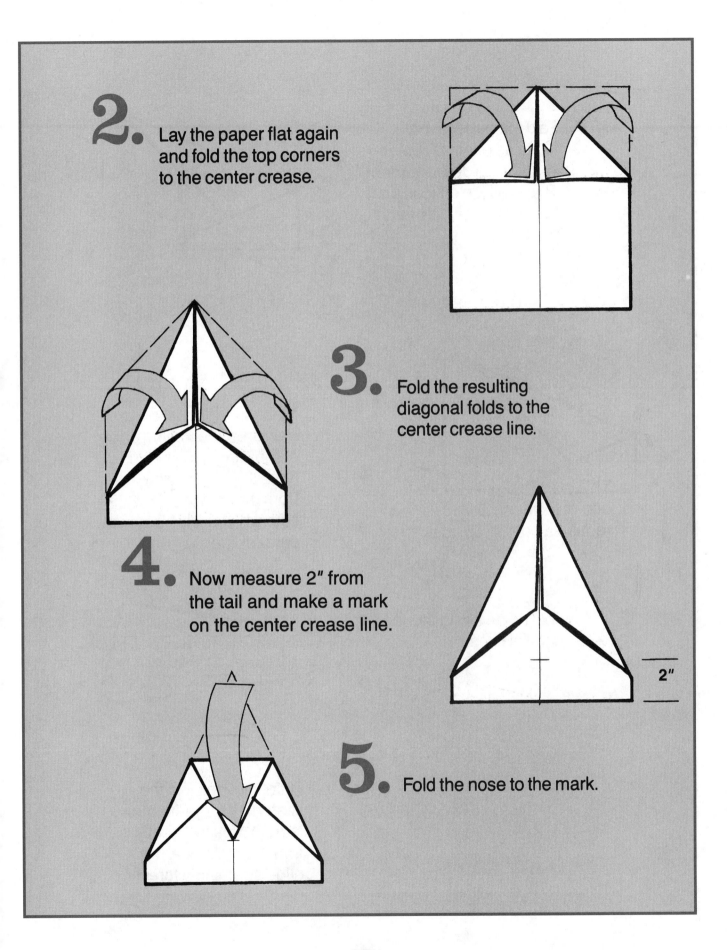

2. Lay the paper flat again and fold the top corners to the center crease.

3. Fold the resulting diagonal folds to the center crease line.

4. Now measure 2" from the tail and make a mark on the center crease line.

2"

5. Fold the nose to the mark.

17

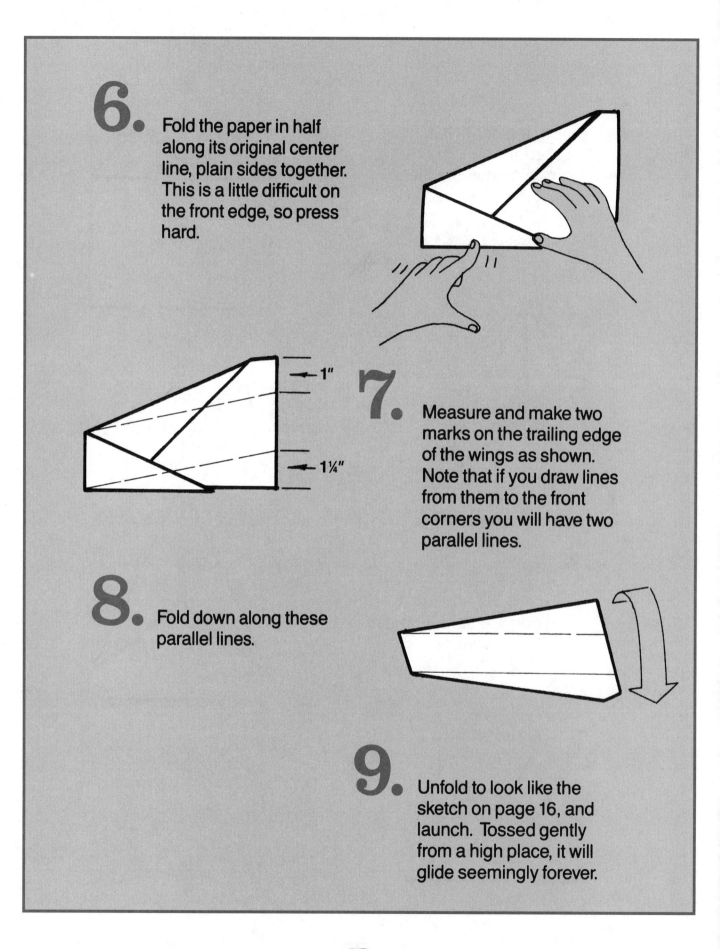

6. Fold the paper in half along its original center line, plain sides together. This is a little difficult on the front edge, so press hard.

← 1"

← 1¼"

7. Measure and make two marks on the trailing edge of the wings as shown. Note that if you draw lines from them to the front corners you will have two parallel lines.

8. Fold down along these parallel lines.

9. Unfold to look like the sketch on page 16, and launch. Tossed gently from a high place, it will glide seemingly forever.

"URUBU" THE BRAZILIAN CONDOR

This model actually does resemble a bird with its wings spread out and it is very easy to make and fly. It requires three paper clips for the nose weight. It is strictly an indoor flyer.

1. Fold an 8½" x 11" piece of paper in half the short way, as shown.

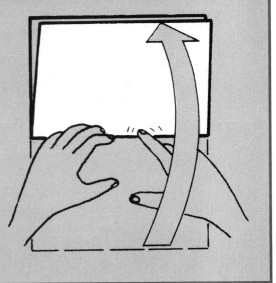

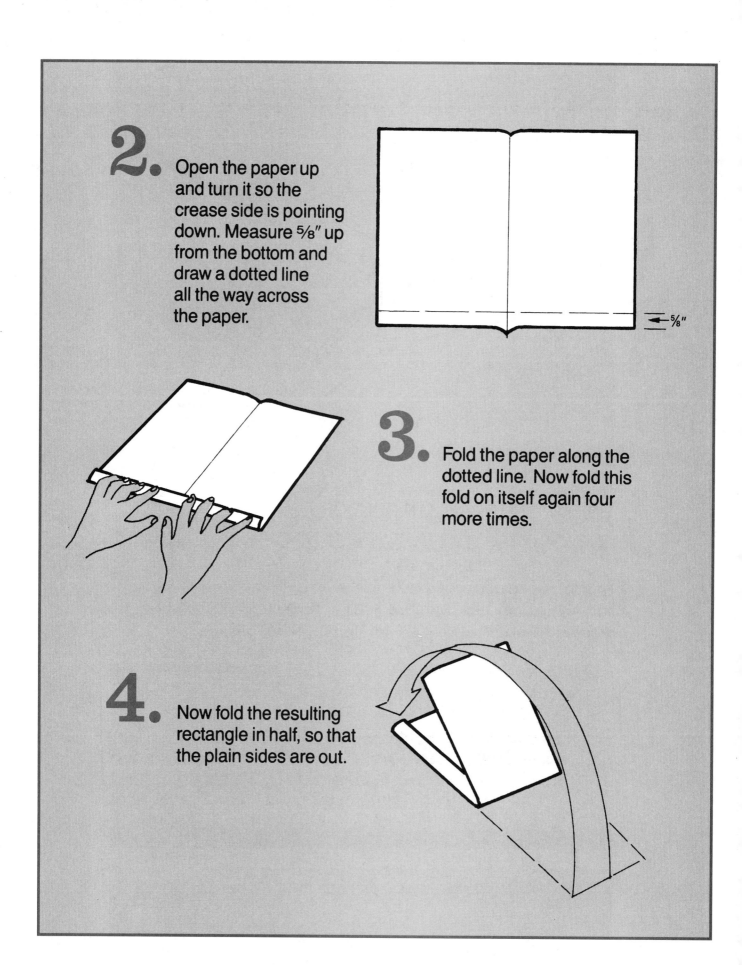

2. Open the paper up and turn it so the crease side is pointing down. Measure 5/8" up from the bottom and draw a dotted line all the way across the paper.

← 5/8"

3. Fold the paper along the dotted line. Now fold this fold on itself again four more times.

4. Now fold the resulting rectangle in half, so that the plain sides are out.

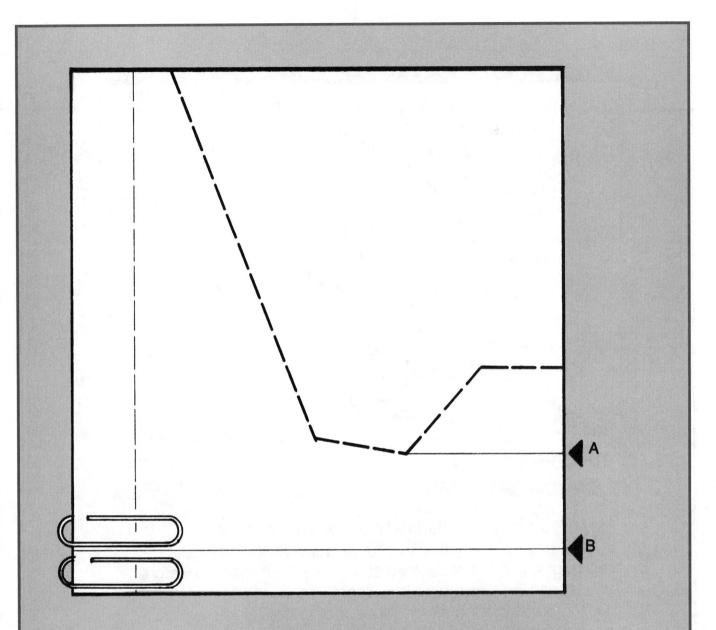

5. Here is your folded piece of paper as it now looks. The light dotted line indicates the inside folds. Cut on the heavy dotted line, as shown in the diagram, to create the wings and the rudder/elevators. Fold down on the fold lines A and B. Place one paper clip below fold line B so that only one side of the center keel is clipped. The "V" shaped keel should open freely. Open your plane and adjust it so that it looks like the finished sketch on page 19.

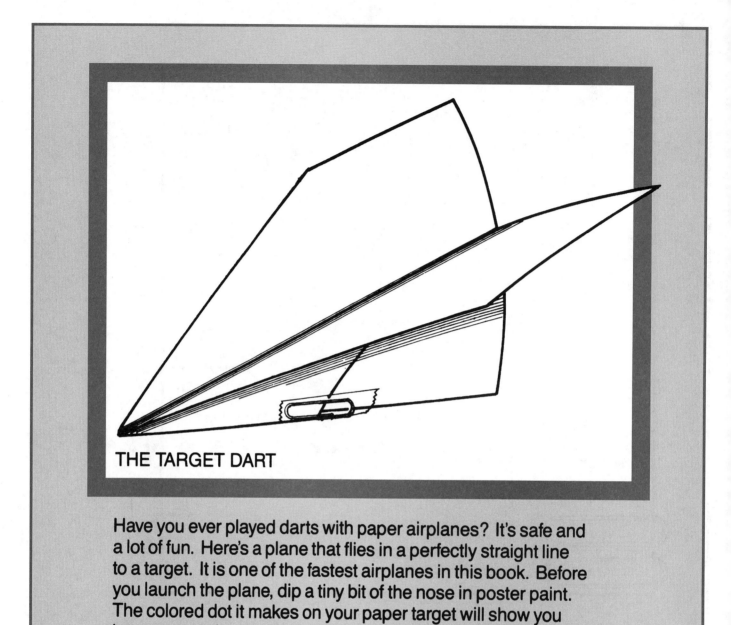

THE TARGET DART

Have you ever played darts with paper airplanes? It's safe and
a lot of fun. Here's a plane that flies in a perfectly straight line
to a target. It is one of the fastest airplanes in this book. Before
you launch the plane, dip a tiny bit of the nose in poster paint.
The colored dot it makes on your paper target will show you
how accurately you can throw.

1. Cut an 8½" x 11" piece
of paper to 8½" x 8½".
Fold it in half.

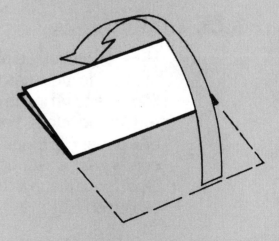

2. Fold the top corner points to the center line so that they are pointing at each other. Make sure the folds taper off to nothing at the bottom corners.

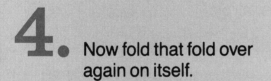

3. Fold the top down to where the corners meet.

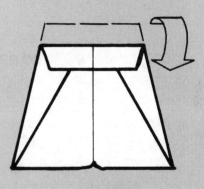

4. Now fold that fold over again on itself.

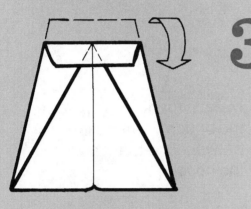

5. Fold the top corners to the center line, as shown on the left.

6. Fold the plane again along its center line, plain sides together, and lay it down, as shown. Tape the bottom as shown.

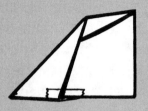

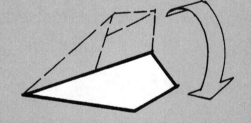

2⅛ "

7. Make a mark 2⅛" up from the bottom. Draw a line between the mark and the nose.

8. Fold the wings down along this dotted line. Open and adjust the wings so that they look like the sketch on page 22. Place a paper clip over the tape. Now it's time for target practice!

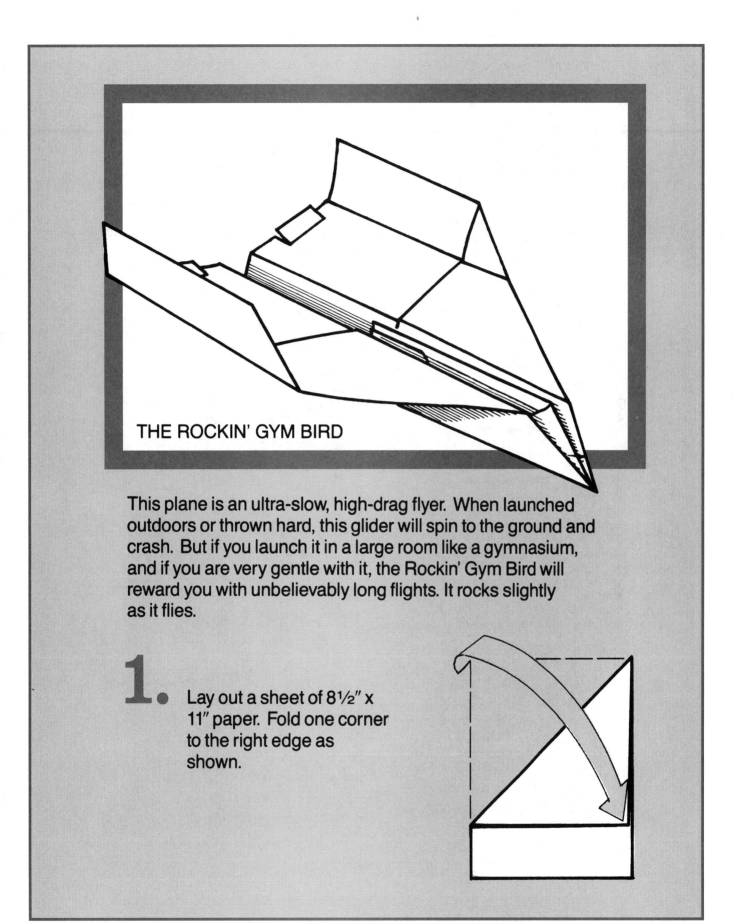

THE ROCKIN' GYM BIRD

This plane is an ultra-slow, high-drag flyer. When launched outdoors or thrown hard, this glider will spin to the ground and crash. But if you launch it in a large room like a gymnasium, and if you are very gentle with it, the Rockin' Gym Bird will reward you with unbelievably long flights. It rocks slightly as it flies.

1. Lay out a sheet of 8½" x 11" paper. Fold one corner to the right edge as shown.

2. Now do the same to the top corner, following the diagram.

3. Fold the paper in half, so that the plain sides are out.

4. Lay it out as shown. Measure 1¼" from the bottom and 1" from the top. These are the fold lines A and B.

A
←1"

B
←1¼"

5. Fold the paper down along fold line B, and up along fold line A. Leave the center fin standing.

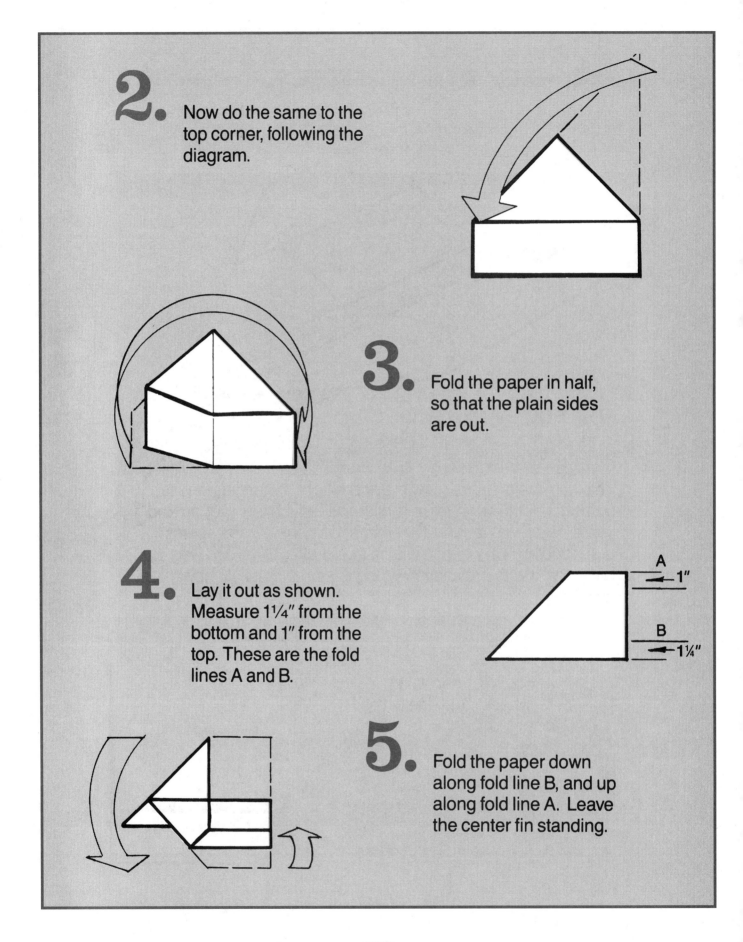

6.

Fold the center fin into the fuselage accordian-style.

7.

Cut short slits for elevators. Your finished plane should look like this:

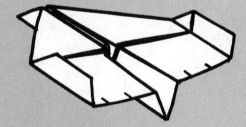

NOTE:
Use no paper clips or staples on this plane. The bent-up wing tips should be tilted slightly outward. Be patient with this one. It's not as easy to fly as the others.

THE FLOATING AERO DART

This plane looks super fast, but in fact it will drift along like a hang glider. It can float almost motionlessly when launched into a slight breeze.

1. Fold an 8½" x 11" piece of paper in half the long way.

2. Now lay the paper flat again and fold the corners to the center crease. The center crease points down as shown.

3. Fold the resulting diagonal folds to the center line.

4. Now your paper looks like this:

5. Turn the plane over and fold it along the center line again so that the plain sides are together.

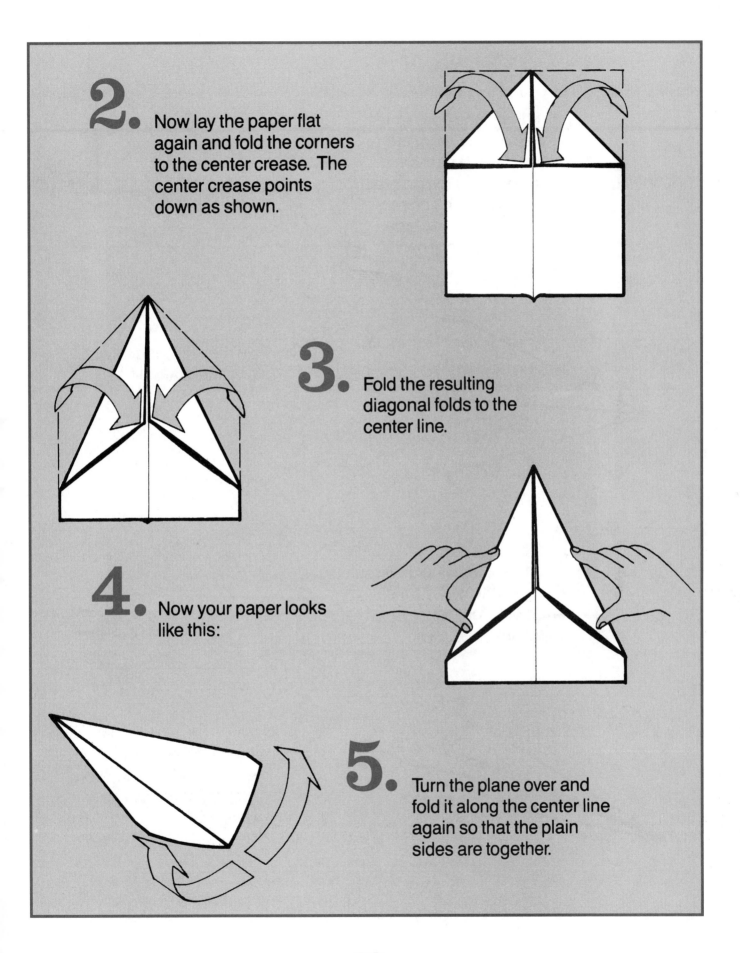

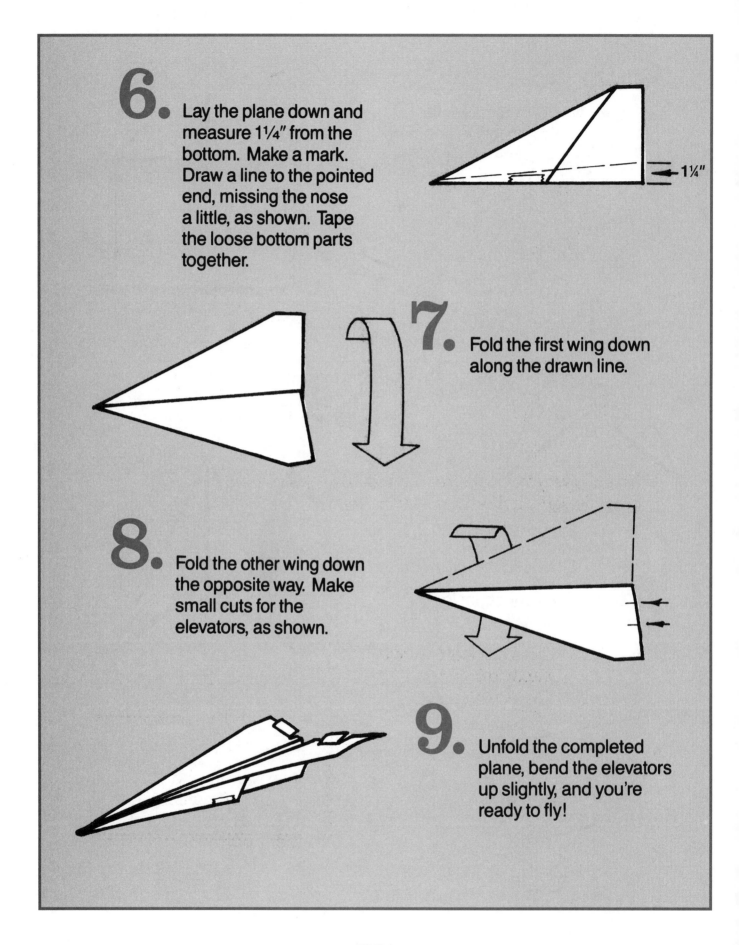

6. Lay the plane down and measure 1¼″ from the bottom. Make a mark. Draw a line to the pointed end, missing the nose a little, as shown. Tape the loose bottom parts together.

←1¼″

7. Fold the first wing down along the drawn line.

8. Fold the other wing down the opposite way. Make small cuts for the elevators, as shown.

9. Unfold the completed plane, bend the elevators up slightly, and you're ready to fly!

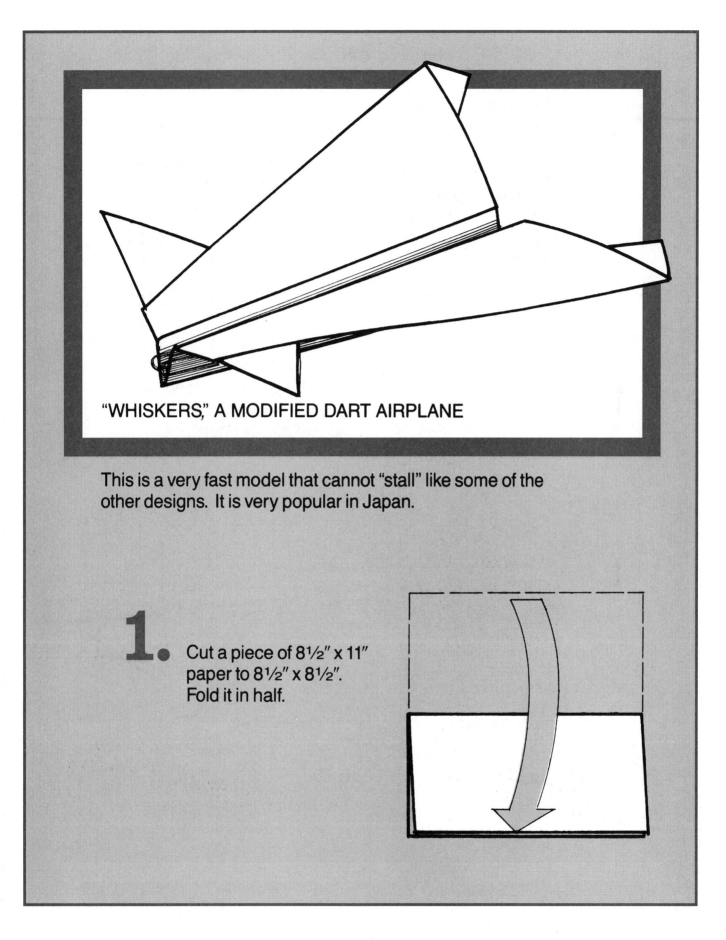

"WHISKERS," A MODIFIED DART AIRPLANE

This is a very fast model that cannot "stall" like some of the other designs. It is very popular in Japan.

1. Cut a piece of 8½" x 11" paper to 8½" x 8½". Fold it in half.

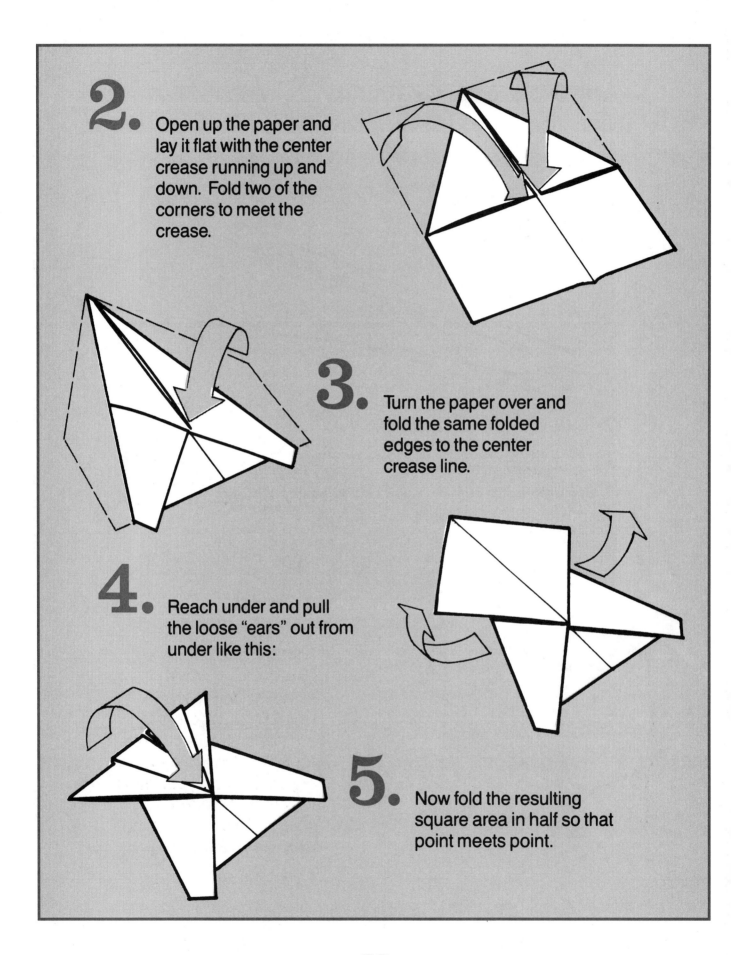

2. Open up the paper and lay it flat with the center crease running up and down. Fold two of the corners to meet the crease.

3. Turn the paper over and fold the same folded edges to the center crease line.

4. Reach under and pull the loose "ears" out from under like this:

5. Now fold the resulting square area in half so that point meets point.

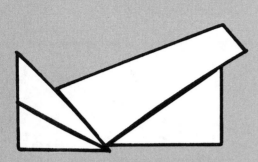

6. Now turn the paper over. Fold the plain sides together along the center crease line.

7. Measure ¾″ up from the bottom and make a mark on both sides. Draw a dotted line across, as shown.

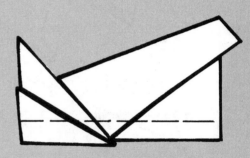

8. Fold first one wing, then the other wing, down along the dotted line. Unfold the plane to look like the finished sketch on page 31. Use two paper clips at the nose, but leave the center "v" open, as shown. This is important!

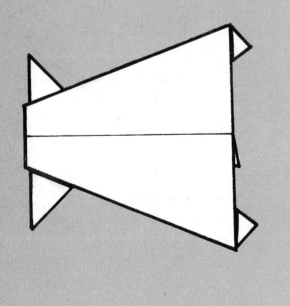

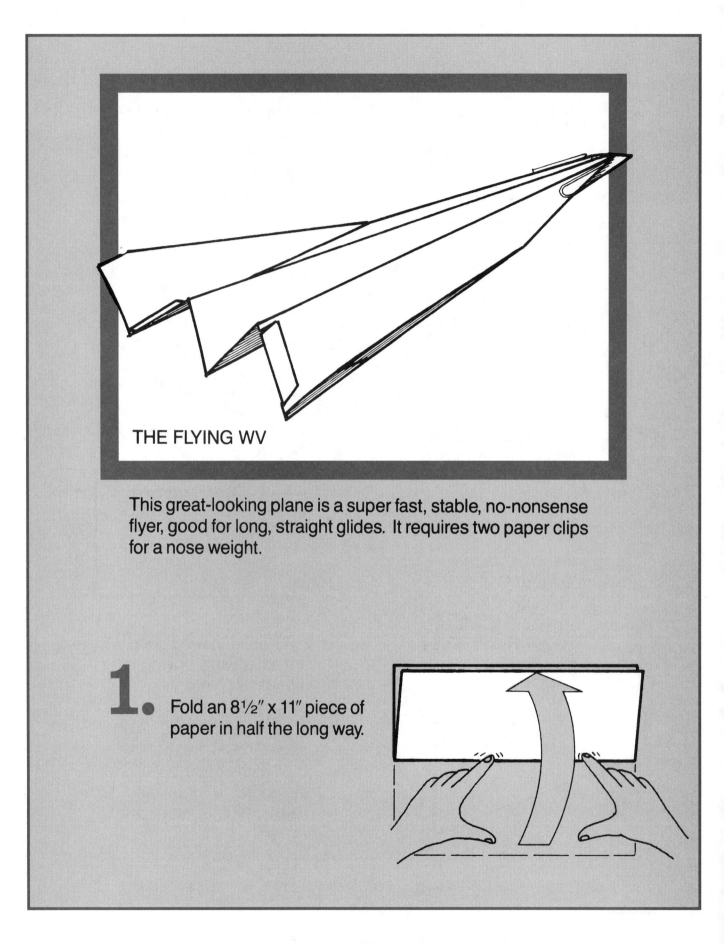

THE FLYING WV

This great-looking plane is a super fast, stable, no-nonsense flyer, good for long, straight glides. It requires two paper clips for a nose weight.

1. Fold an 8½″ x 11″ piece of paper in half the long way.

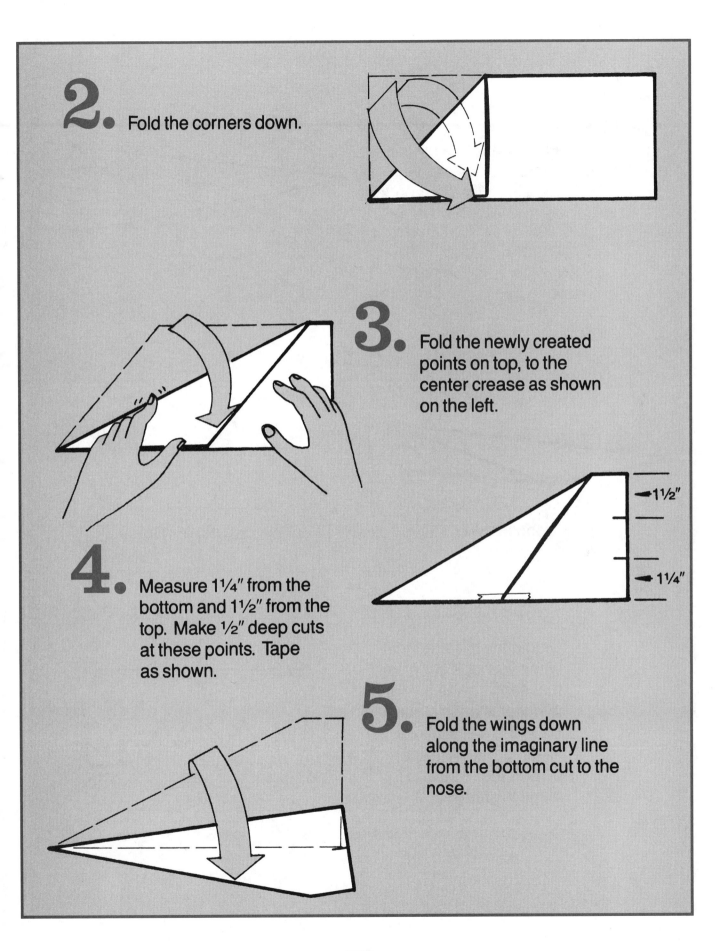

2. Fold the corners down.

3. Fold the newly created points on top, to the center crease as shown on the left.

1½″

1¼″

4. Measure 1¼″ from the bottom and 1½″ from the top. Make ½″ deep cuts at these points. Tape as shown.

5. Fold the wings down along the imaginary line from the bottom cut to the nose.

6. From the 1½″ mark, draw a line that is exactly parallel to the upper edge.

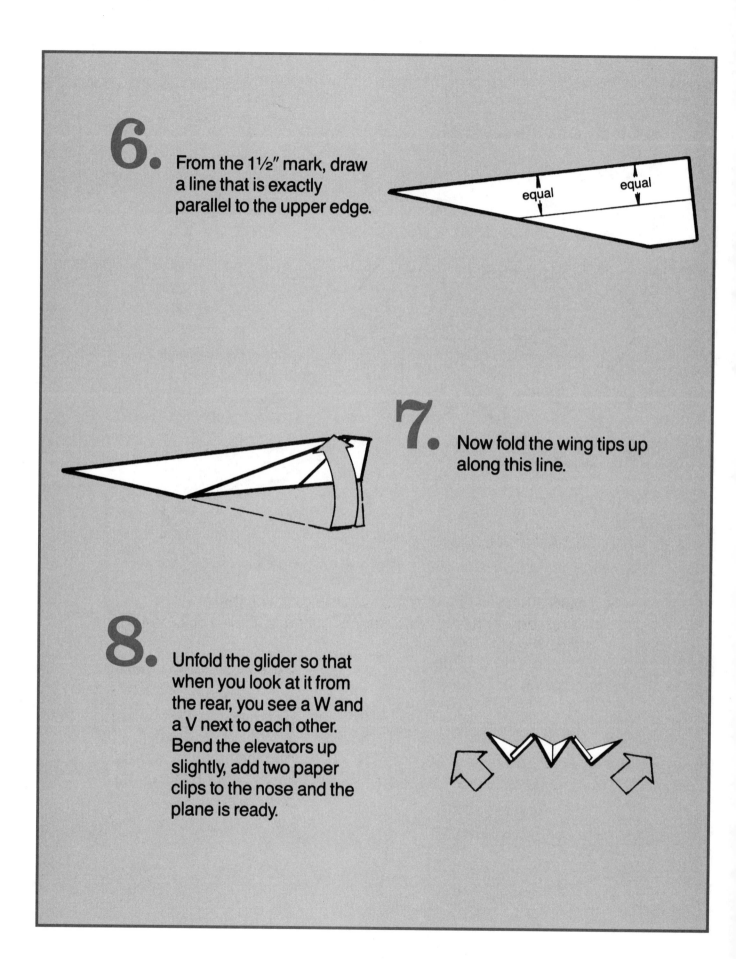

7. Now fold the wing tips up along this line.

8. Unfold the glider so that when you look at it from the rear, you see a W and a V next to each other. Bend the elevators up slightly, add two paper clips to the nose and the plane is ready.

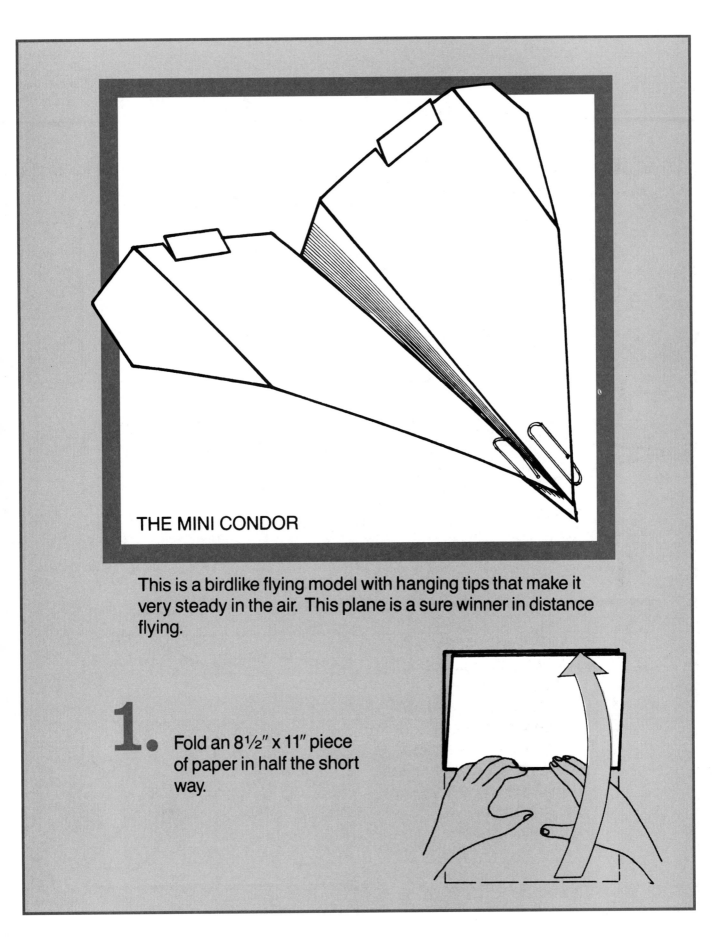

THE MINI CONDOR

This is a birdlike flying model with hanging tips that make it very steady in the air. This plane is a sure winner in distance flying.

1. Fold an 8½″ x 11″ piece of paper in half the short way.

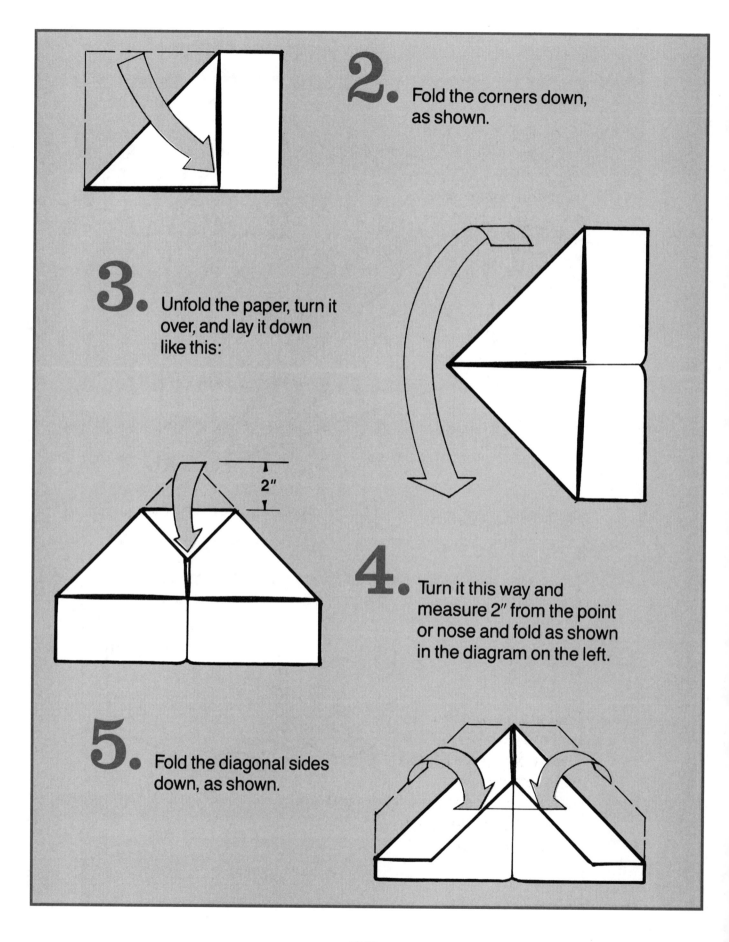

2. Fold the corners down, as shown.

3. Unfold the paper, turn it over, and lay it down like this:

2"

4. Turn it this way and measure 2" from the point or nose and fold as shown in the diagram on the left.

5. Fold the diagonal sides down, as shown.

6. Fold the paper in half along its center line so that the other folds show. Tape the bottom as shown. Measure 1⅜" from the top and 1¼" from the bottom. Make small marks as shown.

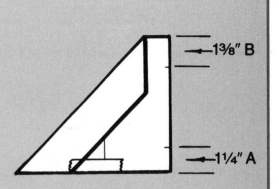

1⅜" B

1¼" A

7. Fold the wings down first along a line from the A mark to the nose. Then fold on the B mark, parallel to the folds you just made. Cut the elevators where shown.

8. Fold the elevators up so that the plane looks like this when seen from the rear. Add two paper clips to the nose and launch. Can you see how much it looks like a condor?

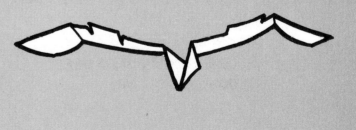

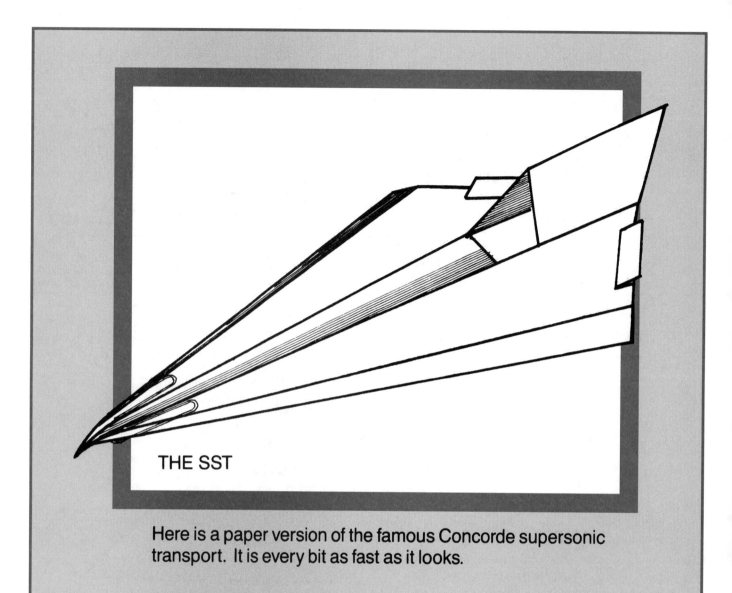

THE SST

Here is a paper version of the famous Concorde supersonic transport. It is every bit as fast as it looks.

1. Cut a piece of 8½″ x 11″ paper to 8½″ x 8½″ square. Fold from corner to corner.

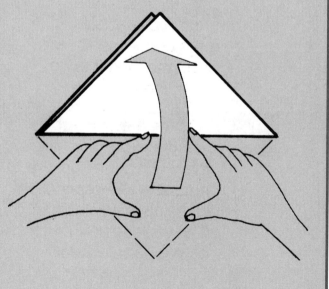

2. Fold one edge down to meet the crease.

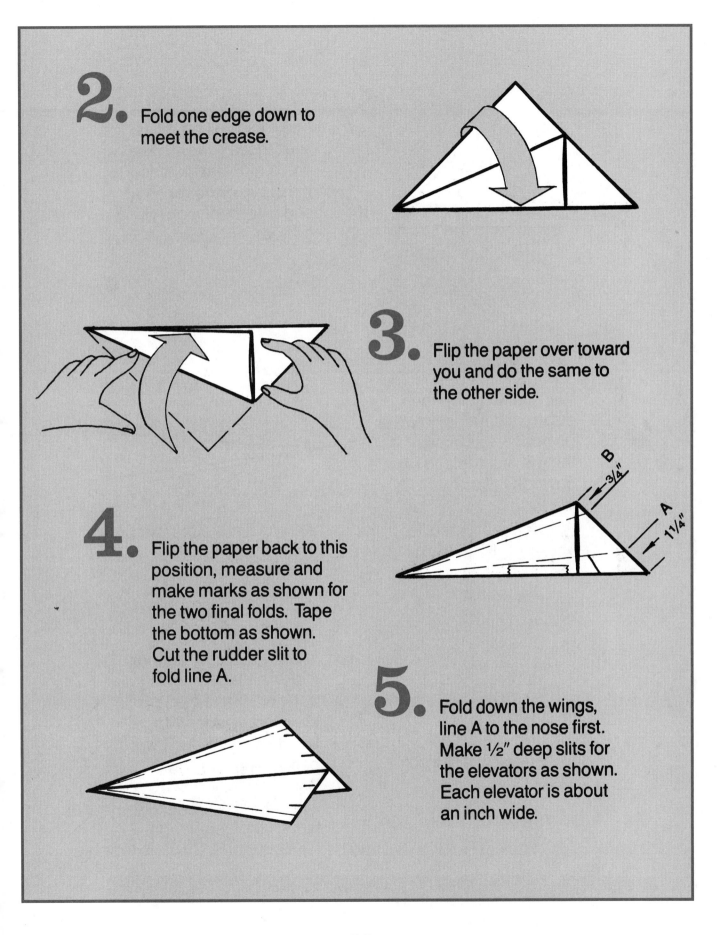

3. Flip the paper over toward you and do the same to the other side.

4. Flip the paper back to this position, measure and make marks as shown for the two final folds. Tape the bottom as shown. Cut the rudder slit to fold line A.

B
3/4"
A
1¼"

5. Fold down the wings, line A to the nose first. Make ½" deep slits for the elevators as shown. Each elevator is about an inch wide.

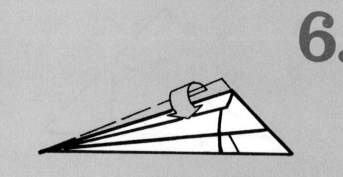

6.

Make folds along the B lines to the nose. These are "slats" that increase the curve of the wings and give them more lifting power.

7.

With the wings opened out, flip the rudder into the up position, as shown. If the wings are folded back down, the plane will look like this:

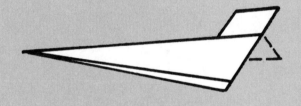

8.

Open the plane. It should look like the sketch on page 40. Bend the elevators up slightly and the slats down. Add two paper clips as shown. Bend the nose down a little. Now you're ready to launch this super model!

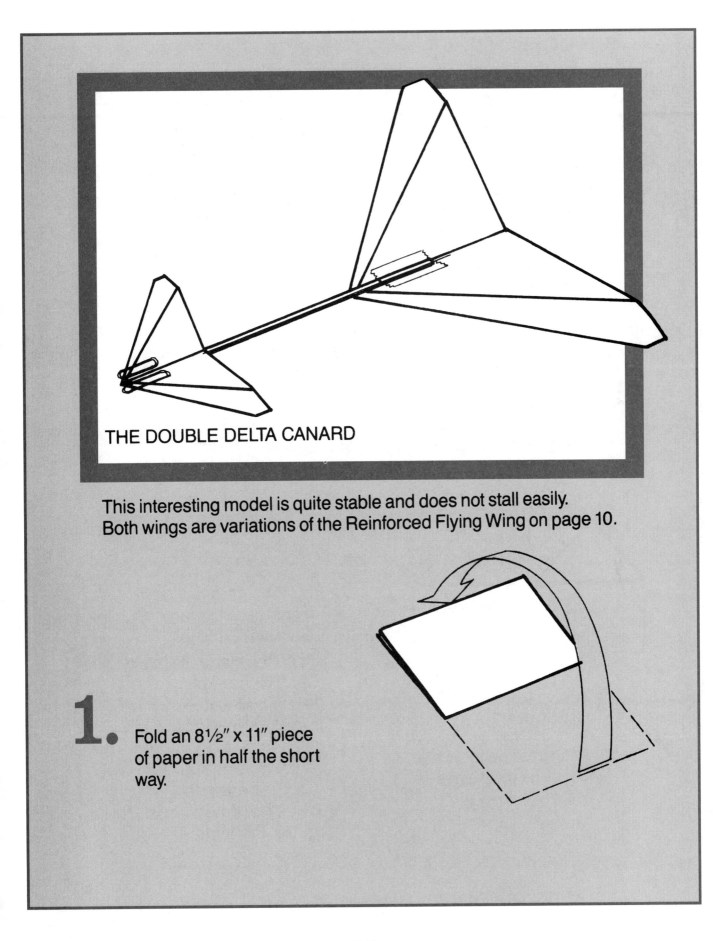

THE DOUBLE DELTA CANARD

This interesting model is quite stable and does not stall easily.
Both wings are variations of the Reinforced Flying Wing on page 10.

1. Fold an 8½″ x 11″ piece of paper in half the short way.

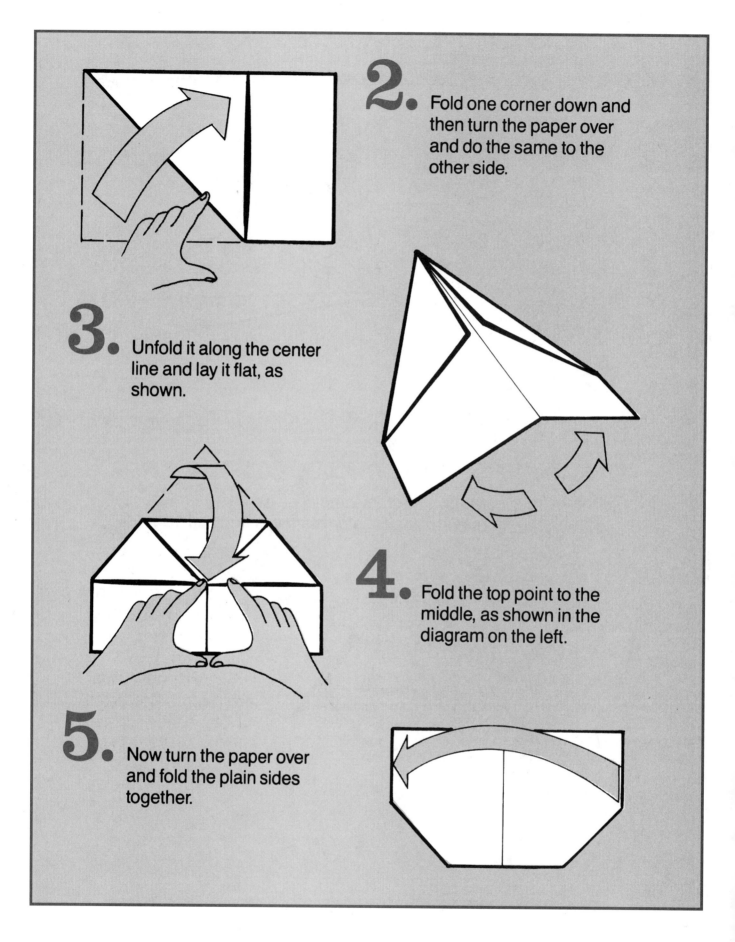

2. Fold one corner down and then turn the paper over and do the same to the other side.

3. Unfold it along the center line and lay it flat, as shown.

4. Fold the top point to the middle, as shown in the diagram on the left.

5. Now turn the paper over and fold the plain sides together.

6. Now follow steps 6 through 9 on page 12, eliminating the folding and bottom mark completely. Unfold it so that it looks like the rear or main wing in the sketch on page 43. This wing has no folded center keel or rudder, only the center crease.

Follow the same process for the front wing or stabilizer except that you will use a piece of paper cut to 4⅞″ x 6¼″.

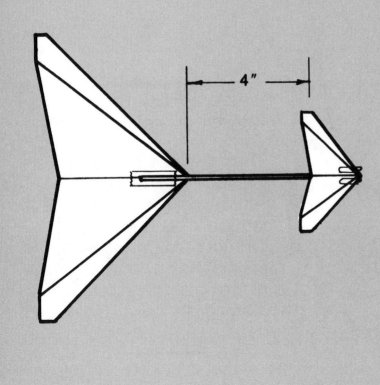

4″

7. Connect the pieces with a soda straw or a bamboo skewer. Tape above the rear wing and below the front stabilizer, as shown. Add two paper clips to the front stabilizer. Note: A third clip next to the others may be necessary.

THE PARASOFTY

This parachute is terrific fun. You can tie any small action figure or lightweight toy to the threads to serve as the parachutist. If your friends are making it too, have contests to see whose parachute floats the longest.

1. Take a two-ply paper dinner napkin, unfold it and lay it out flat.

2. Cut two pieces of heavy sewing thread, each 24″ long. Attach them by tying the ends of each piece of thread to the opposite corners of the napkin.

3. Hold all of the corners together and let the threads hang down as shown.

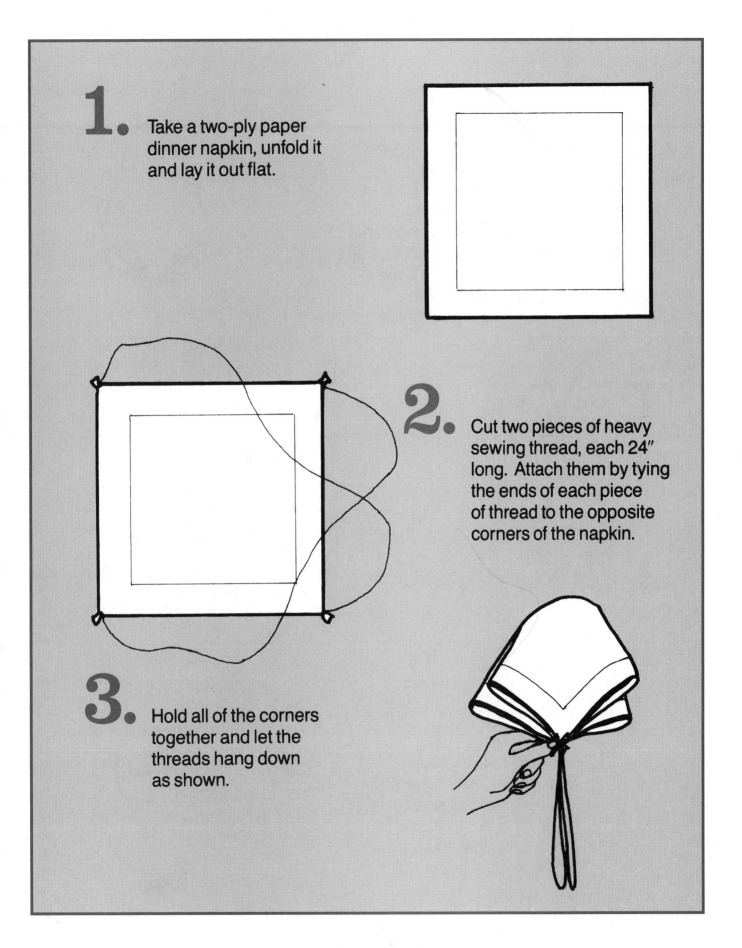

4. Tie the weight you have chosen to the dangling loops of thread. Be sure that all four pieces of thread are carrying some of the weight, and that no one thread is too loose when you hold the parachute from the top.

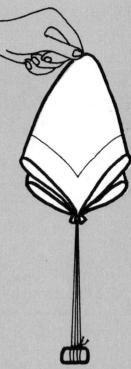

5. Fold the gathered napkin over once and then again. Wind the threads loosely around the bundle of folded napkin.

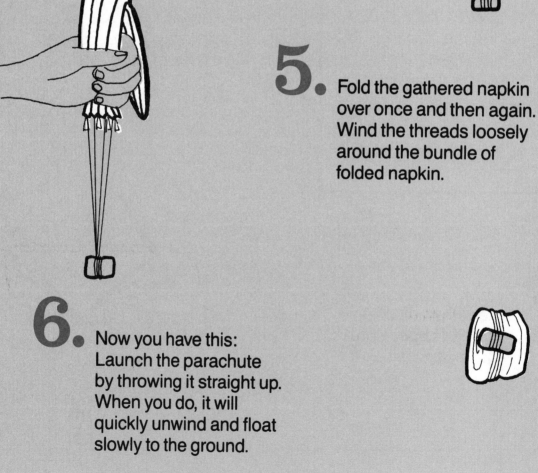

6. Now you have this: Launch the parachute by throwing it straight up. When you do, it will quickly unwind and float slowly to the ground.

THE DYNAMIC DART

Here is a good floating airplane that soars through the air with the help of a slight breeze. It is a variation of the Floating Aero Dart but the Dynamic Dart has a heavier nose, which makes it fly faster.

1. Fold an 8½" x 11" piece of paper in half the long way.

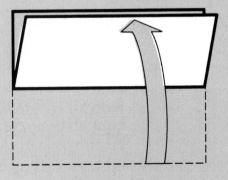

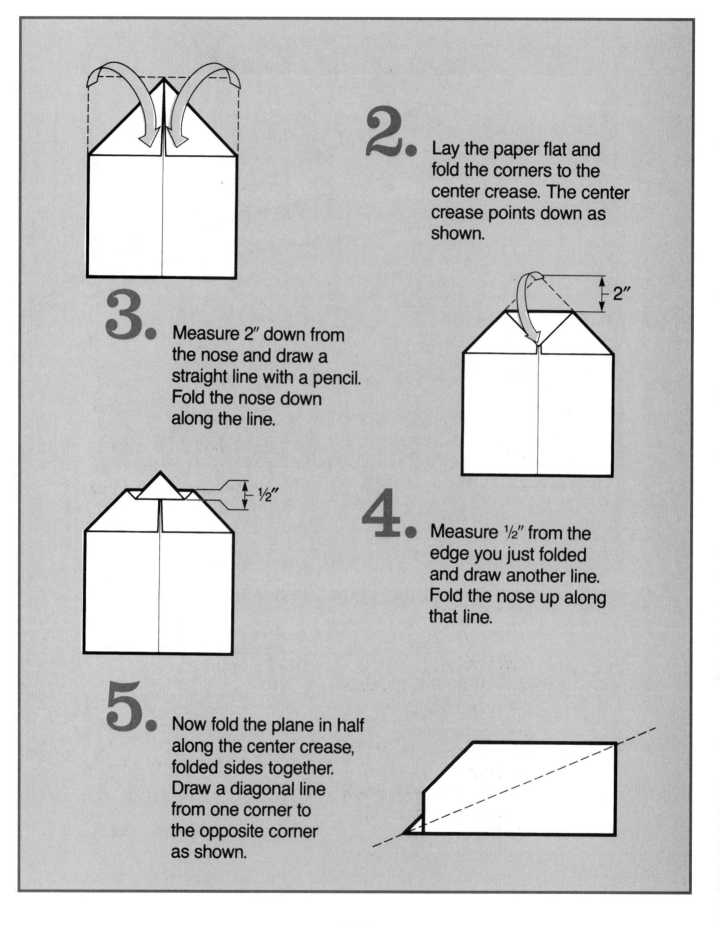

2. Lay the paper flat and fold the corners to the center crease. The center crease points down as shown.

2"

3. Measure 2" down from the nose and draw a straight line with a pencil. Fold the nose down along the line.

4. Measure ½" from the edge you just folded and draw another line. Fold the nose up along that line.

½"

5. Now fold the plane in half along the center crease, folded sides together. Draw a diagonal line from one corner to the opposite corner as shown.

6. Fold both wings down along the line in opposite directions.

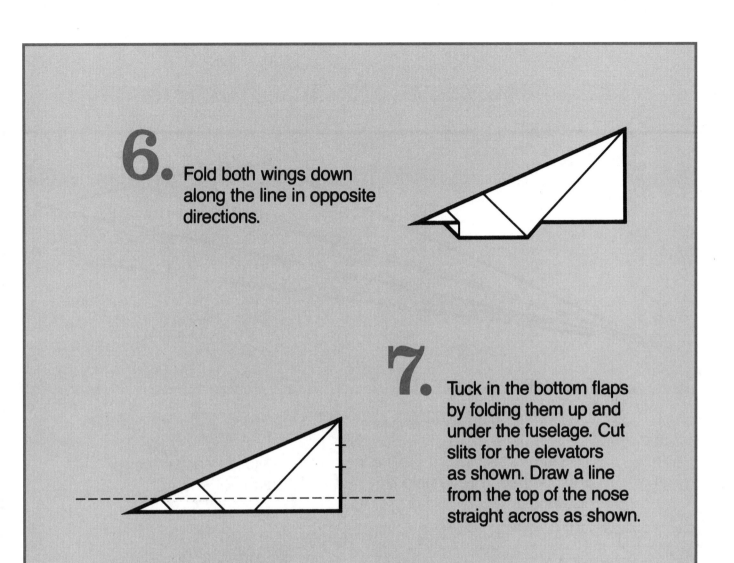

7. Tuck in the bottom flaps by folding them up and under the fuselage. Cut slits for the elevators as shown. Draw a line from the top of the nose straight across as shown.

8. Fold both wings down along the line in opposite directions. Clip all the pieces together by attaching a paper clip to the bottom. Unfold and adjust your plane to look like the sketch on page 49. Bend the elevators up and you're ready to go!

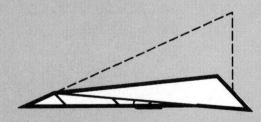

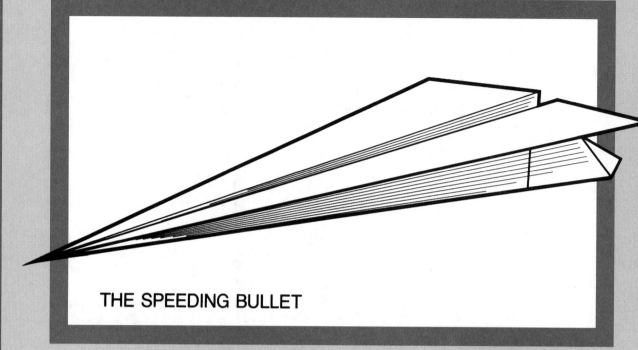

THE SPEEDING BULLET

This sleek, streamlined plane is easy to make. Its narrow wings and compact design help it fly fast and straight for short distances.

1. Fold an 8½" by 11" piece of paper in half the short way.

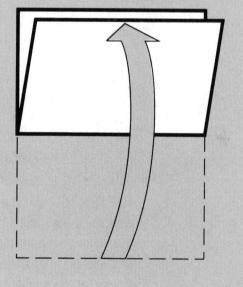

2. Lay the paper flat and fold the top corners halfway toward the center crease.

equal distance

3. Fold the new corners to the center crease. The bottom corners should overlap.

4. Now fold the new edges to the center crease.

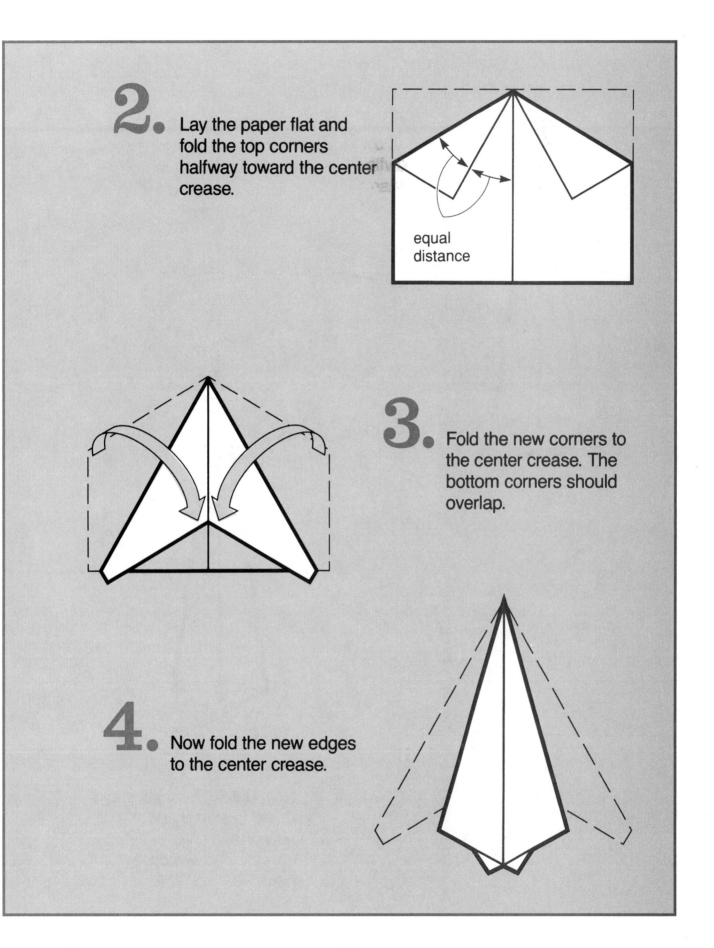

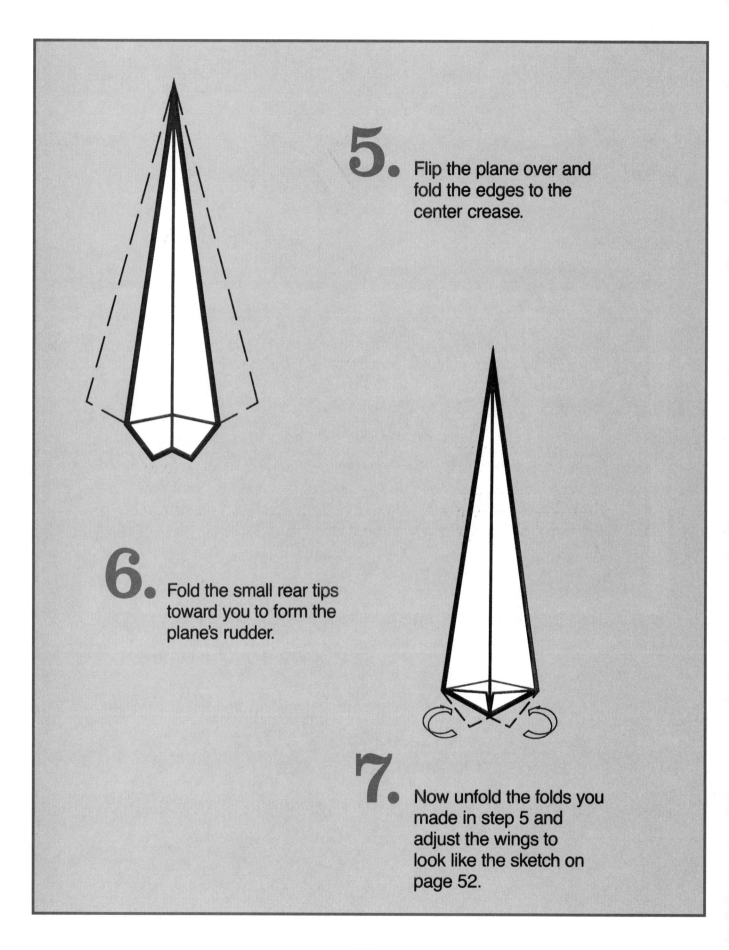

5. Flip the plane over and fold the edges to the center crease.

6. Fold the small rear tips toward you to form the plane's rudder.

7. Now unfold the folds you made in step 5 and adjust the wings to look like the sketch on page 52.

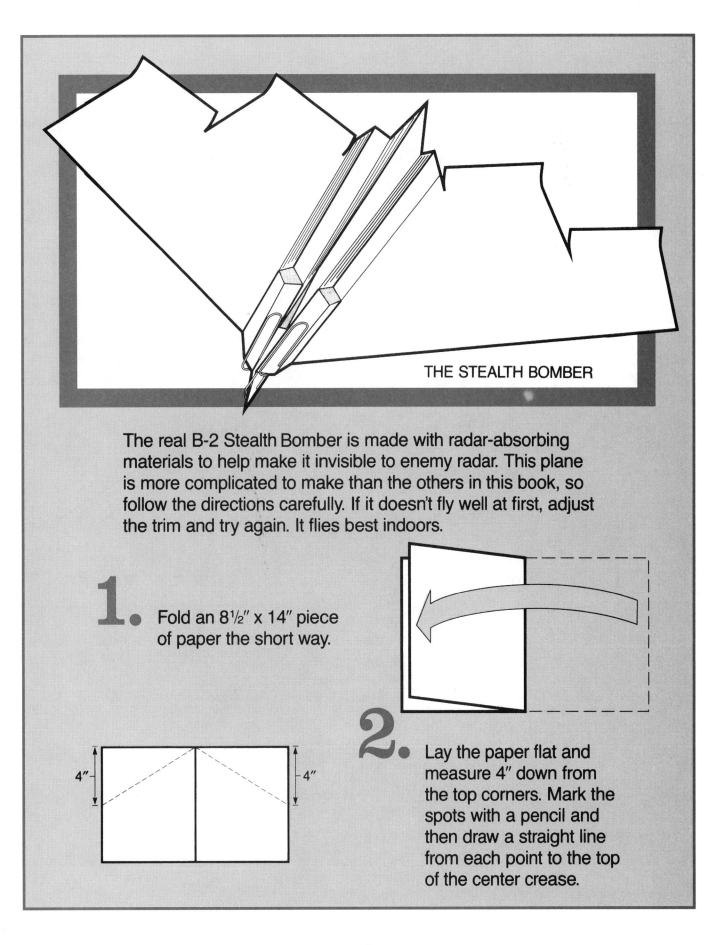

THE STEALTH BOMBER

The real B-2 Stealth Bomber is made with radar-absorbing materials to help make it invisible to enemy radar. This plane is more complicated to make than the others in this book, so follow the directions carefully. If it doesn't fly well at first, adjust the trim and try again. It flies best indoors.

1. Fold an 8½″ x 14″ piece of paper the short way.

2. Lay the paper flat and measure 4″ down from the top corners. Mark the spots with a pencil and then draw a straight line from each point to the top of the center crease.

3. Fold the top corners down on the line.

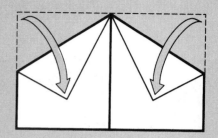

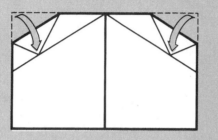

4. Unfold and lay flat. Fold the top corners to the folds you made in the previous step.

5. Fold the new edges over on the existing creases and tape them down. Now you need to create the pattern for the wings. Measure 1″ from the side and 2″ from the bottom. Make a dot with a pencil to mark the spot. Then measure 2½″ from the side and 3″ from the bottom and make a dot. Make another dot 4″ from the side and 1″ from the bottom. Now make a dot 6″ from the side and 2″ from the bottom. Finally, make a dot 1″ from the bottom on the center crease.

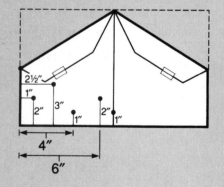

6. Connect the dots using a pencil and ruler.

7. Cut along the lines you drew.

8. Now fold the plane along the center crease and trace along the cut edge on the opposite wing. Cut the wing along the lines you drew.

9. Measure ½″ from the wide edge and draw a line. Turn the plane so the point with a star is facing you.

½″

10. Fold both wings down in opposite directions along the line you drew. Then fold each wing up along the dotted line as shown.

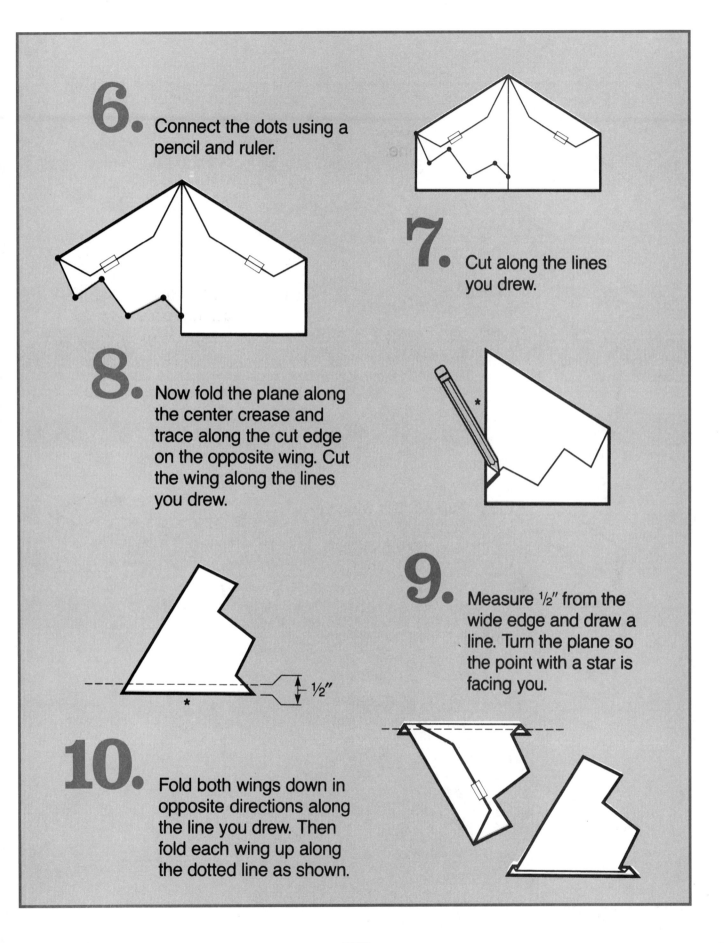

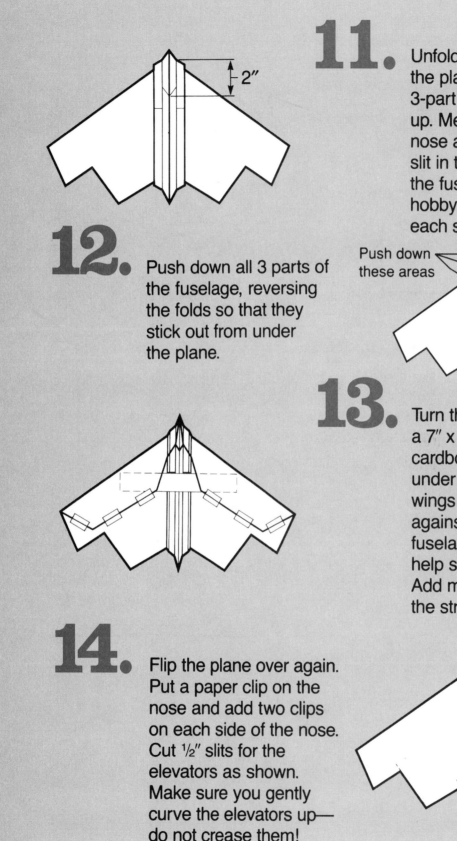

11. Unfold the wings and lay the plane flat so that the 3-part fuselage is face-up. Measure 2″ from the nose and cut a diagonal slit in the middle part of the fuselage using a hobby knife. Cut a slit on each side of the fuselage.

Push down these areas

12. Push down all 3 parts of the fuselage, reversing the folds so that they stick out from under the plane.

13. Turn the plane over. Cut a 7″ x 1″ strip of thin cardboard. Slip the strip under the two taped wings so that it butts up against the two side fuselage slits. This will help stabilize the wings. Add more tape to hold the strip in place.

14. Flip the plane over again. Put a paper clip on the nose and add two clips on each side of the nose. Cut ½″ slits for the elevators as shown. Make sure you gently curve the elevators up—do not crease them!

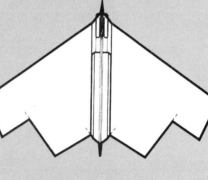

58

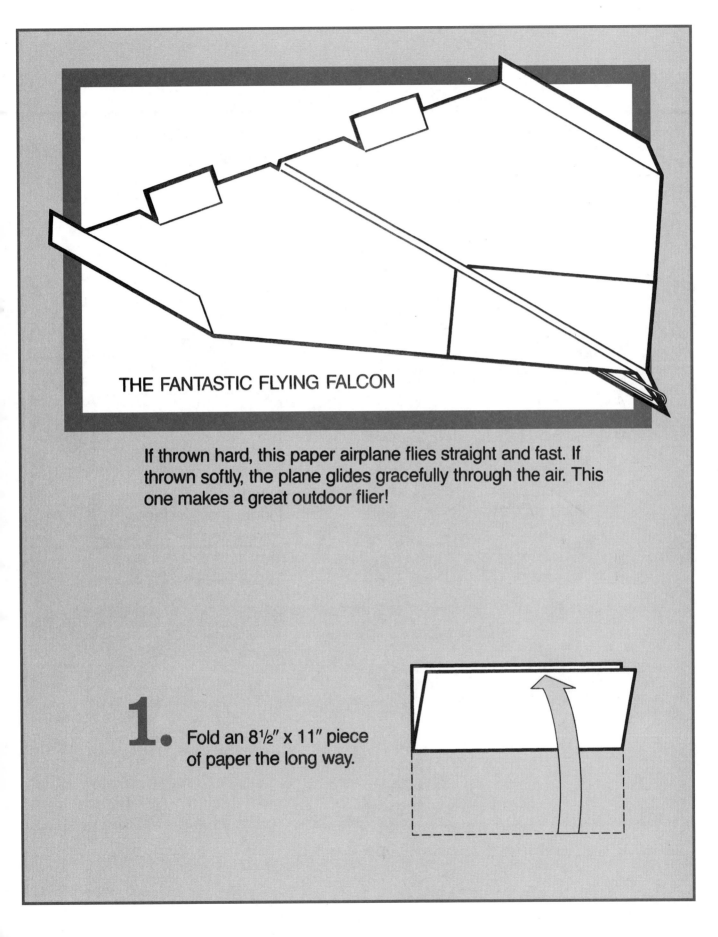

THE FANTASTIC FLYING FALCON

If thrown hard, this paper airplane flies straight and fast. If thrown softly, the plane glides gracefully through the air. This one makes a great outdoor flier!

1. Fold an 8½" x 11" piece of paper the long way.

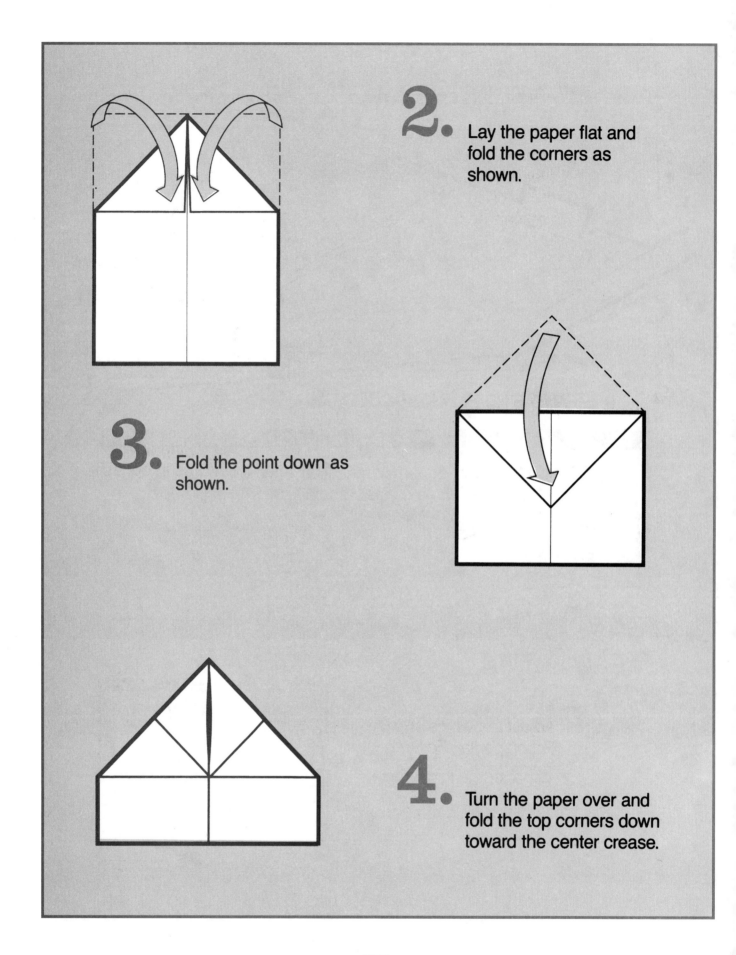

2. Lay the paper flat and fold the corners as shown.

3. Fold the point down as shown.

4. Turn the paper over and fold the top corners down toward the center crease.

5. Turn the paper over again and fold it in half. Measure about ½″ from the left side and draw a vertical line as shown.

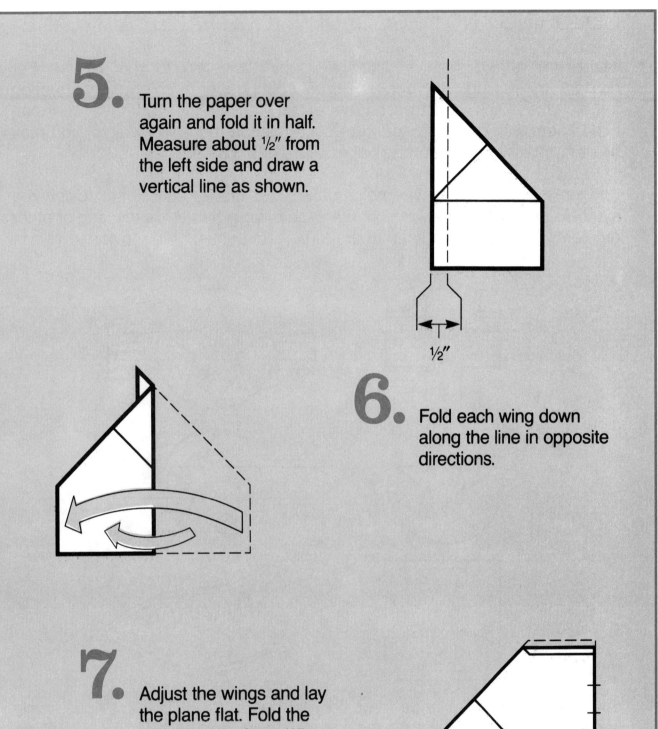

½″

6. Fold each wing down along the line in opposite directions.

7. Adjust the wings and lay the plane flat. Fold the wing tips up about ¼″. Cut small slits for the elevators. Put a paper clip on the nose, bend the elevators up, and get ready for takeoff!

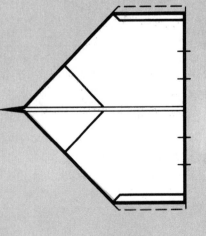

COLORING AND DECORATING YOUR PAPER AIRPLANE

There are various ways you can add color and flair to your planes. For starters, try making them out of colored typing paper or colored construction paper. Use black construction paper for the Stealth Bomber. You can experiment with origami paper, but because it is more lightweight, you may need to attach more than one paper clip to the fuselage.

Emblems and symbols will help make your plane look better. Copy the symbols below onto the wings or fuselage of your plane. Try thinking of other emblems you may have seen at the airport, in books, or in movies.

You can also draw fancy patterns on your plane using circles, stripes, wavy lines, or whatever you want! Use green, brown, and olive for a camouflage pattern. Magic markers or colored pencils work best. Paint may make your plane too heavy, and crayons may be too hard to work with. Here are some examples to follow.

FLYING TIPS

THE RUDDER

By creating a rudder, you can make your plane turn left or right. The rudder is always at the rear of the fuselage. Here's how to make a rudder:

1. Measure no more than ½″ up from the bottom of the fuselage and make a small cut.

2. To make your plane turn right, bend the rudder to the right.

3. To make your plane turn left, bend the rudder to the left.

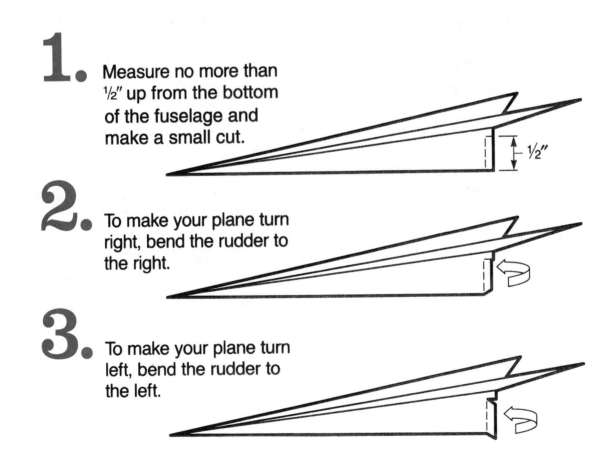

To get the best control, the elevators on your plane should be bent equally to each other no matter which way the rudder is bent. The more you bend the rudder, the sharper the plane will turn. Your plane may also dive more steeply. To keep your plane from diving too steeply, make sure the elevators are bent all the way up.

PAPER CLIPS

As you know, attaching paper clips to the nose or fuselage will help balance your plane. You can experiment by moving the clip back an inch or more from the nose. If the plane crashes, just change its center of gravity by putting the clip in another place. Now try again!

If your plane flies nose up and then stalls and crashes, try adding a paper clip or some tape to the nose. You can also try bending the elevators down. If the plane then starts nose diving, take off some of the nose weight.

THE NOSE KNOWS

When you're flying paper airplanes, the nose almost always gets smashed when it hits the ground or other object. To help avoid this, you can wind a piece of cellophane or transparent tape around the nose to protect it. Don't use too much tape or you'll make the plane too heavy.

ELEVATORS AND AILERONS

You already know about cutting elevators on your plane to change the shape of the wings and provide more lift. Try bending one elevator up and the other down. Can you predict what will happen when the plane flies? Launch it and see if you're right. Now see what happens if you bend the elevators halfway up, and then try again with the elevators bent all the way up. By experimenting, you can learn the effect different changes have on the plane's flight patterns.

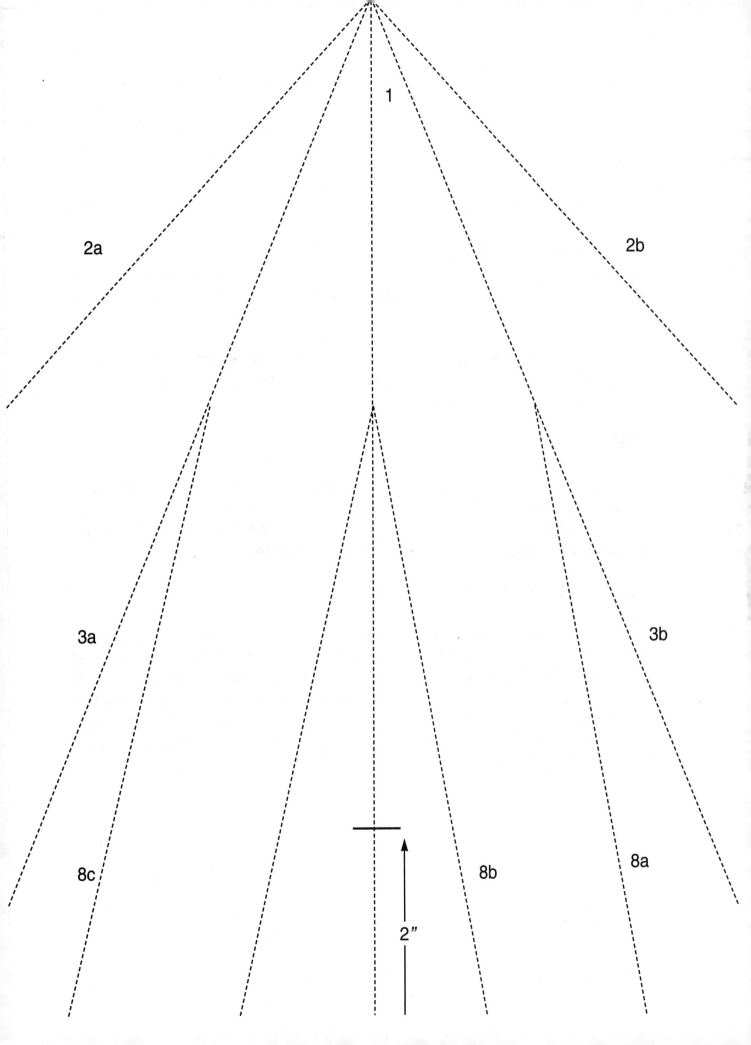

2a

2b

1

3a

3b

8c

8b

8a

2"

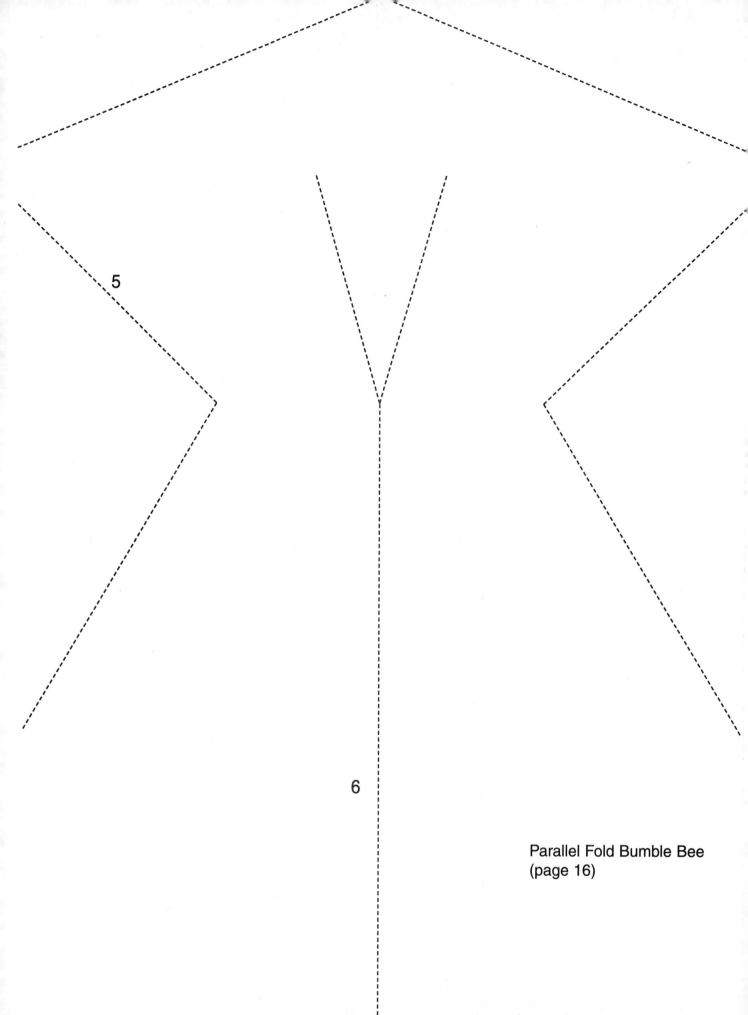

5

6

Parallel Fold Bumble Bee
(page 16)

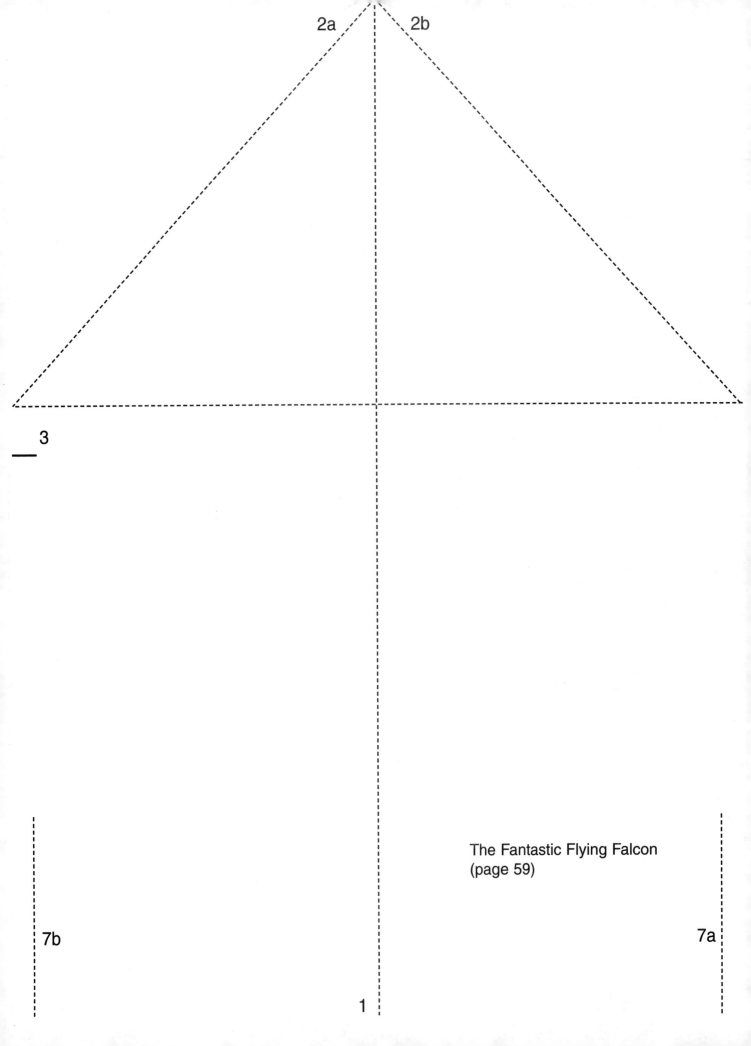

2a   2b

3

The Fantastic Flying Falcon
(page 59)

7b   7a

1

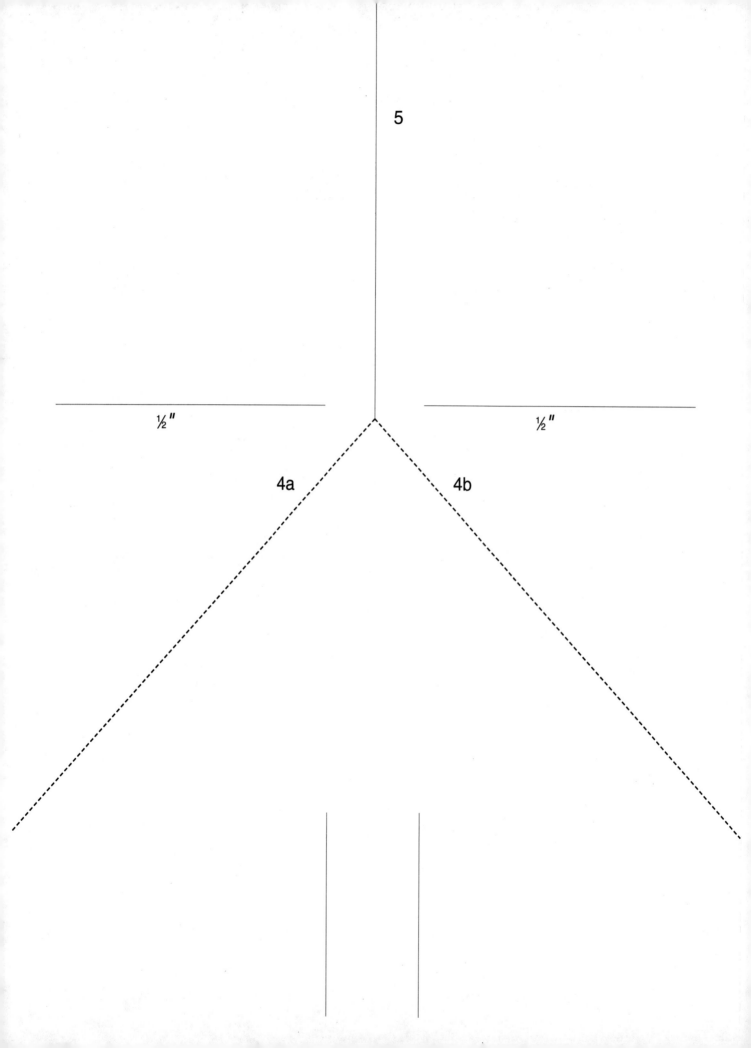

5

½"   ½"

4a   4b